THE AMERICAN PEOPLE

The American People In the Depression

Edited by
DAVID KENNEDY

James Axtell, Series Editor

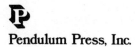

Pendulum Press, Inc.

West Haven, Connecticut

Published by
Pendulum Press, Inc.
The Academic Building
Saw Mill Road
West Haven, Connecticut 06516

Printed in the United States of America

Cover Design by Dick Brassil, Silverman Design Group

CONTENTS

ABOUT THE EDITOR

David Kennedy graduated with honors in history from Stanford University and has an M.A. and a Ph.D. from Yale University. Currently an Assistant Professor of history at Stanford, Mr. Kennedy teaches courses in Twentieth-Century United States, American Intellectual History, and American Studies. He has published several books and articles among which are: *Birth Control in America: The Career of Margaret Sanger*, *Progressivism: The Critical Issues* (editor), and "World War I and Vietnam: A Comparison of Their Impact on America."

ABOUT THE SERIES EDITOR

James Axtell, the recipient of a B.A. degree from Yale University and a Ph.D. from Cambridge University, has also studied at Oxford University and was a postdoctoral fellow at Harvard University. Mr. Axtell has taught history at Yale and is currently Associate Professor of Anglo-American History at Sarah Lawrence College. He is on the editorial board of *History of Education Quarterly* and has been a consultant to the American Council of Learned Societies. He has published several articles and reviews and is the author of a forthcoming book, *The School upon a Hill: Education and Society in Colonial New England.*

ACKNOWLEDGMENTS

Grateful acknowledgment is made to the authors and publishers who granted permission to reprint the following selections:

The American Worker in the Twentieth Century, by Eli Ginzberg and Hyman Berman, reprinted by permission of The Macmillan Company. Copyright © The Free Press of Glencoe, 1963.

" 'Buy Now'—on $30 a Week," by James R. Martin from *The Nation,* November 1, 1933. Reprinted by permission.

"The CCC Marches Toward a New Destiny," by Frank Ernest Hill. Copyright © 1937 by the New York Times Company. Reprinted by permission.

The Christian Century, September 18, 1935, reprinted by permission of The Christian Century Foundation. Copyright © 1935.

"A Crisis for Our Youth: a Task for the Nation," by Aubrey Williams, Copyright © 1936 by the New York Times Company. Reprinted by permission.

Fortune Magazine, October 10, 1934, reprinted by permission of *Fortune Magazine.*

"Half Slave, Half Free: Unemployment, the Depression, and American Young People," by George R. Leighton and Richard Hellman, reprinted by permission of the authors and *Harper's Bazaar Magazine.* Copyright © The Hearst Corporation.

Hard Times: An Oral History of the Great Depression, by Studs Terkel. Copyright © 1970 by Studs Terkel. Reprinted by permission of Pantheon Books/A Division of Random House, Inc.

Middletown in Transition, by Robert S. and Helen M. Lynd. Copyright © 1937 by Harcourt, Brace and Jovanovich, Inc. Reprinted by permission of the Publishers.

"Mr. Lewis and the Auto Strike," from *The New Republic,* February 3, 1937.

"On the Assembly Line," by Gene Richard, reprinted by permission of *The Atlantic Monthly,* April 1937.

Research Memorandum on the Family in the Depression, by Samuel A. Stouffer and Paul F. Lazarsfelt. Reprinted by permission of the Social Science Research Council.

"Sitting Down in Flint," by Bruce Bliven, from *The New Republic,* January 27, 1937. Reprinted by permission of the author.

The Unemployed, by Eli Ginzberg, by permission of Harper and Row, Inc.

FOREWORD

The American People is founded on the belief that the study of history in the schools and junior levels of college generally begins at the wrong end. It usually begins with abstract and pre-digested *conclusions*—the conclusions of other historians as filtered through the pen of a textbook writer—and not with the primary sources of the past and unanswered *questions*—the starting place of the historian himself.

Since we all need, use, and think about the past in our daily lives, we are all historians. The question is whether we can be skillful, accurate, and· useful historians. The only way to become such is to exercise our historical skills and interests until we gain competence. But we have to exercise them in the same ways the best historians do or we will be kidding ourselves that we are *doing* history when in fact we are only absorbing sponge-like the results of someone else's historical competence.

Historical competence must begin with one crucial skill—the ability to distinguish between past and present. Without a sharp sense of the past as a different time from our own, we will be unable to accord the people of the past the respect that we would like to receive from the people of the future. And without according them that respect, we will be unable to recognize their integrity as individuals or to understand them as human beings.

A good sense of the past depends primarily on a good sense of the present, on experience, and on the imaginative empathy to relate ourselves to human situations not our own. Although most students have had a relatively brief experience of life and have not yet given full expression to their imaginative sympathies, they do possess the one essential prerequisite for the study of history—the lives they have lived from birth to young adulthood. This should be the initial focus of their study of the past, not remotely adult experiences to which they cannot yet relate, such as politics, diplomacy, and war.

Thus the organizing perspective of this series is the universal life experiences that all people have: being born, growing up, loving and marrying, working and playing, behaving and misbehaving, worshipping, and dying. As only he could, Shakespeare portrayed these cycles in *As You Like It* (Act II, scene vii):

> All the world's a stage,
> And all the men and women merely players.
> They have their exits and their entrances;
> And one man in his time plays many parts,
> His acts being seven ages. At first the infant,
> Mewling and puking in the nurse's arms.
> And then the whining school-boy, with his satchel
> And shining morning face, creeping like snail
> Unwillingly to school. And then the lover,
> Sighing like furnace, with a woeful ballad
> Made to his mistress' eyebrow. Then a soldier,
> Full of strange oaths, and bearded like a pard;
> Jealous in honour, sudden and quick in quarrel,
> Seeking the bubble reputation
> Even in the cannon's mouth. And then the justice,
> In fair round belly with good capon lined,
> With eyes severe and beard of formal cut,
> Full of wise saws and modern instances;
> And so he plays his part. The sixth age shifts
> Into the lean and slipper'd pantaloon,
> With spectacles on nose and pouch on side;
> His youthful hose, well saved, a world too wide
> For his shrunk shank; and his big manly voice,
> Turning again toward childish treble, pipes
> And whistles in his sound. Last scene of all,
> That ends this strange eventful history,
> Is second childishness, and mere oblivion,
> Sans teeth, sans eyes, sans taste, sans everything.

These are experiences to which any student can relate and from which he can learn, simply because they surround him daily in his home, community, and not least, school.

There is an additional reason for focussing on the universal life cycle. If history is everything that happened in the past, obviously some things were and are more important than others. Until fairly recently the things historians have found important have been the turning points or *changes* in history—"great" men and "great" events. But recently, with the help of anthropologists, historians have come to a greater awareness of the importance of stability and inertia, of *non*-change in society. For every society—and therefore its history—is a mixture of change and stability, of generally long periods of fixity punctuated now and then by moments of modification and change.

The major reason for the stability of society is the conservative bent of human behavior and ideals, the desire to preserve, hold, fix, and keep stable. People acquire habits and habits impede change. The habits people acquire are the common ways the members of a society react to the world—how they behave and feel and think in common—which distinguish them from other societies and cultures. So at bottom history is about ordinary people, how they did things alike and together that gave continuity and durability to their society so that it could change to meet new circumstances without completely losing its former identity and character.

America is such a society and *The American People* is an attempt to provide representative selections from primary sources about the lives and habits of ordinary people in periods of history that are usually known in textbooks for their great changes.

Since the experience of each student is the only prerequisite for the study of primary sources at the first level, annotations and introductory material have been reduced to a minimum, simply enough to identify the sources, their authors, and the circumstances in which they were written.

But the remains of the past are mute by themselves. Many sources have survived that can tell us what happened in the past and why, but they have to be questioned properly to reveal their secrets. So by way of illustration, a number of questions have been asked in each chapter, but these should be supplemented by the students whose experiences and knowledge and interests are, after all, the flywheel of the educational process. Although the questions and sources are divided into chapters, they should be used freely in the other chapters; the collection should be treated as a whole. And although most of the illustrative questions are confined to the sources at hand, questions that extend to the present should be asked to anchor the acquired knowledge of the past in the immediate experience of the present. Only then will learning be real and lasting and history brought to life.

INTRODUCTION

"We in America today are nearer to the final triumph over poverty than ever before in the history of any land," said Herbert Hoover as he accepted the Republican presidential nomination in 1928. "We have not reached the goal," he went on, "but . . . we shall soon, with the help of God, be in sight of the day when poverty will be banished from this nation." Few prophecies have been as sadly mistaken as that one, for beginning in 1929, the first year of Hoover's Presidency, the Great Depression fell on the United States like a deadly plague. It was to last twelve years, until the outbreak of World War II, and it left scars on the American people that have not yet entirely disappeared.

It is difficult today to realize just how terrible a shock the Great Depression was. We know that by the end of Hoover's term in office, in 1933, Gross National Product had fallen to three fourths of its 1929 level, and that it did not regain that level until America entered the Second World War in 1941. We know that more than 5,000 banks, holding the savings of hundreds of thousands of people, failed between 1929 and 1933, and that, at least on paper, investors in the stock market lost nearly 80 *billion* dollars in those four years. And we know that, by 1933, one worker in every four was unemployed. As late as 1939, one out of six persons who sought jobs could not find them. Millions of people who had considered themselves hardworking, respectable, even modestly prosperous, suddenly found themselves without work, without self-respect, and without money. Poverty became a "normal" experience in the world's richest country.

These facts are familiar. They all indicate that the Great Depression, in both magnitude and duration, was a painful trauma for American society. But statistics can reveal only a glimpse of the misery the Depression brought into the lives of individual men, woman, and young people. The documents in this collection go beneath the "large" view, and show the personal effects of twelve years of poverty and broken hopes.

The dictionary defines "trauma" as "a startling experience which has a lasting effect on mental life; a shock." That is a useful definition with which to approach the selections that follow. What, exactly, do they show that was "startling," or new, about the circumstances of people's lives in the 1930s? Had the previous decade, the 1920s, left people especially unprepared for economic hardship? How did they live with unexpected poverty and uncertainty? What kinds of effects did the Depression have on people's mental lives? Did it affect their identity, their sense of personal worth? What effects did it have on their relationships with each other, especially within the family? Did it influence people's sex lives? Their religious beliefs?

We should pay special attention to the "lasting effects" of the Depression. In what ways did it affect people's basic values? Did it, for example, alter their attitude toward money and material things? Toward economic security? Did it change ideas about morality, about what was right and what was wrong? Did it shake people's faith in the country, their faith in democracy and capitalism? Did it change attitudes toward authority? Toward the government? Toward work? Toward planning for the future?

We should also examine how the Depression affected different people in different ways. Did it have the same impact, for example, on men and on women, on the young and the old, blacks and whites, city-dwellers and farmers, or on working-class wage-earners and the salaried middle classes? What do the different reactions to the Depression say about the structure of American society, the way society defines different roles for its various members?

Finally, we should try to get a sense of the 1930s as history, by asking ourselves how that decade is different from the present. Could a similar depression occur today? If it did, would people react in the same way? Have the relative positions of different groups in the society changed? To what extent are those changes due to the Depression? What difference does it make to grow up in an impoverished age, rather than an affluent one? Are people's values and attitudes today different from what they were in the 1930s? If so, in what ways is the memory of the Depression responsible for those differences? How has the Depression of the 1930s affected *your* life, forty years later?

PROLOGUE: TRYING TO IMAGINE . . .

Everybody has heard about the Depression, from parents, or grandparents, or from books. But what was it really like? How did it affect the details of people's lives, the things we usually take for granted? Would it be different today? The three young people in the conversation below are trying to imagine.

This conversation is reprinted from Studs Terkel's Hard Times: An Oral History of the Great Depression *(New York: Pantheon, 1970), 22-23. Terkel, a journalist, interviewed hundreds of people in the 1960s on the subject of the Depression. Some of them had lived through it; others, like Lily, Roy, and Bucky knew about it only indirectly. His book, which consists of transcripts of the taped interviews, is a fascinating collection of first-hand memories and impressions.*

LILY, ROY AND BUCKY

Lily is eighteen. Her brother, Roy, is sixteen. Bucky is seventeen. They are of lower middle-class families.

LILY: My grandmother'd tell us things about the Depression. You can read about it, too. What they tell us is different than what you read.

ROY: They're always tellin' us that we should be glad we got food and all that, 'cause back in the Thirties they used to tell us people were starving and got no jobs and all that stuff.

LILY: The food lines they told us about.

ROY: Yeah, you had to stay in line and wait for food.

LILY: And everything. You got when it was there. If it wasn't, then you made without it. She said there was a lot of waiting.

BUCKY: I never had a Depression, so it don't bother me really.

ROY: From what you hear, you'd hate to live in that time.

BUCKY: Well, I ain't livin' in that time.

ROY: We really don't know what it would be like. It seems like a long time ago.

LILY: There's a time I remember bein' hungry. Livin' away from home. I didn't have anybody to depend on. (Indicates the others.) But they didn't leave home. They stay home where it's at.

ROY: Like little things when you're home: where's the butter? There's no butter, you go out and buy it. But like them people: where's the butter? No butter, you gotta wait till you get the butter.

LILY: Maybe it was margarine.

ROY: Now you just walk into your house and sit down, turn on the TV, walk out into the kitchen, get a glass of milk or somethin', watch a football game, baseball game for a few hours. They couldn't do that. If they were hungry and there was nothin' there, they'd just have to wait.

BUCKY: When my parents talk: you should be glad and happy that we got all this now. The clothes you're wearin', the food we eat and all that stuff.

LILY: They used to tell us about this one silver dollar that they had. Whenever they ran out, it was this silver dollar they used to take down to the little shop on the corner and get a dollar's worth of food. They'd give the silver dollar. The guy'd hold it for 'em and when they got a dollar of currency, they could take it in and get their silver dollar back.

I think we'd hurt more now if we had a Depression. You don't see how they'd make it if it happened to 'em again. Because they take a lot of things for granted. I mean, you see 'em now and they have everything. You can't imagine how they would act if they didn't have it. If they would even remember what they did. 'Cause they're past it now. They already done it, and they figure they're over it. If we fell now, I think everybody would take it a lot harder.

Everybody'd step on each other. They'd just walk all over and kill each other. They got more than they ever need that they'd just step on anybody to keep it. They got cars, they got houses, they got this and that. It's more than they need, but they *think* they need it, so they want to keep it. Human life isn't as important as what they got.

I. BIRTH

One way for a family to stretch its income in hard times is to have fewer children. Does the following table indicate that many families responded in this way to the Depression of the 1930s? In what year does the birth rate begin to fall? Nineteen-thirty was the first full year of the Depression. Does that year show a significant change in the birthrate? Why do you think the birthrate may have started to rise again in 1934?

The table on page 22 is from Samuel A. Stouffer and Paul F. Lazarsfeld Research Memorandum on the Family in the Depression *(New York: Social Science Research Council, 1937), 123.*

America is often considered a homogeneous, even conformist, society. But in the 1930s, at least, racial and regional backgrounds accounted for significant differences in life-style, even from the moment of birth. What difference, for example, did it make for a baby to be born in the city or in the country? In the North or in the South? To be born black or white? Which babies had the best chances for survival?

ESTIMATED NUMBER OF BIRTHS, AND
BIRTHS PER 1000 WOMEN AGED 15 TO 44 YEARS:
UNITED STATES, 1920-1935

Year	Estimated Births (Thousands)*	Estimated Number of Women 15-44 (Thousands)**	Estimated Births per 1000 Women 15-44
1920	2851	25,000	114.0
1921	2956	25,400	116.4
1922	2792	25,800	108.2
1923	2824	26,260	107.5
1924	2893	26,700	108.4
1925	2829	27,100	104.4
1926	2767	27,570	100.4
1927	2733	28,000	97.6
1928	2612	28,500	91.6
1929	2525	28,900	87.4
1930	2565	29,300	87.5
1931	2460	29,600	83.1
1932	2400	29,800	80.5
1933	2278	30,100	75.7
1934	2373	30,300	78.3
1935	2359	30,500	77.3

From The Child *2 (September, 1937), 59-60.*

URBAN AND RURAL VARIATIONS

Of the 2,155,105 infants born alive in 1935 in the United States, according to census figures, 1,157,773 (54 percent) were born in rural areas and 997,332 (46 percent) were born in cities with 10,000 or more population. Physicians attended 81 percent of the births in rural areas as compared with 95 percent of the births in cities. Midwives attended 17 percent of the births in rural areas and 3 percent of the births in cities. Of the births in rural areas only 11 percent occurred in hospitals as compared with 67 percent of the births in cities.

Of the 120,138 infant deaths in the United States in 1935, 66,299 (55 percent) occurred in rural areas and 53,839 (45 percent) in cities. The infant mortality rate in 1935 in rural areas was 57 per 1,000 live births as compared with 54 in urban areas. Prior to 1929 urban rates were higher than rural. Infant mortality rates in both urban and rural areas have decreased but the rate of decrease has been significantly faster in urban than in rural areas. The decrease in both urban and rural districts has been largely due to reduction in mortality from gastrointestinal diseases but the rate of decrease has been greater in the cities than in country districts.

VARIATIONS BETWEEN NEGROES AND WHITES

Each year more than 250,000 Negro infants are born alive in the United States. In 1935, of the 2,155,105 live births registered, 1,888,012 (88 percent) were white infants and 255,124 (12 percent) were Negro infants. Almost two-thirds of these Negro infants were born in rural areas of the South, but in every large southern city and in many large northern cities many Negro infants are born each year.

Of the Negro live births in 1935, 56 percent were attended by midwives and 43 percent by physicians. Only 17 percent of the Negro live births occurred in hospitals. Of the white live births 94 percent were attended by physicians (40 percent by physicians in hospitals).

The results of special research on infant and maternal mortality among Negroes, based on statistics issued by the Bureau of the Census and on statistics from the special study of causes of stillbirth in hospitals are especially pertinent in relation to the maternal and child-health programs being developed under the Social Security Act. Practically all States with large Negro populations are giving special attention to the problems of mortality among Negro infants and mothers.

The mortality rate of Negro infants in the United States, 1933-35, was 86 per 1,000 live births as compared with 53 for white infants. In every State with 500 or more Negro live births annually the mortality rate of Negro infants was in excess of that for white infants. In the District of Columbia and 2 States the mortality rate of Negro infants was more than double, and in 18 other States more than 50 percent higher than, that for white infants. More than half of the deaths among Negro infants occurred in the first month of life. The neonatal mortality rate for Negro infants was 45 per 1,000 live births as compared with 32 for white infants. Mortality rates from every type of cause were higher among Negro infants than among white infants. The mortality among Negro infants in each period of the first year of life decreased greatly during the period 1915-35, but the 1933 rates were practically as high as those for white infants in the earliest years of record.

An old proverb tells us that "the poor get poorer," and the following selection seems to confirm that adage. It also shows that the Depression could have a brutal impact even on the lives of small children. What did it mean to Tom, the black sharecropper's child? How did it affect his education? What kind of lasting effect do you think this experience would have on his later life? How different was the experience of Tom's older brother, the "prosperity" child?

From Eli Ginzberg and Hyman Berman, The American Worker in the Twentieth Century: A History Through Autobiographies *(New York: The Free Press, 1963), 215-17.*

Tom is a sharecropper's child, black, in Alabama. His family (father, mother, and four children old enough to make "hands") all work for the landowner, are all collectively continually in debt to him (they get $75 worth of supplies for the growing season and he keeps the books), and all live in a two-room cabin furnished by the landowner. . . .

Tom . . . is now twelve and old enough to be counted by the Census. (The Census enumeration begins at age ten.) But even six years ago in the year of the last Census Tom was at work, though officially nonexistent, along with the thousands of his little fellow laborers, at age six, beginning to pick cotton.

Tom gets up, or is pulled out of bed, at four o'clock in summer, by his older brother, who is quicker than he to hear the landlord's bell. Work for the entire plantation force is "from can see to can't see" (i.e., from daylight to dark), and the bell is their commanding timepiece. The "riding boss"—what a foreman is to a doffer in a textile mill—sees to that. Little Jenny, aged five, is being left at home today to care for the baby, because it is so hot; on cooler days the baby is carried along to the field and laid on a pallet under the tree, and Jenny can play among the cotton rows with the other children who are too young to work. (There are plantations where mothers of young infants are given fifteen minutes nursing time, no more, morning and afternoon. Then they must take the baby along: there is not enough time to go home.)

Tom is a good, steady chopper and can do over half a man's work. At picking he can do two-thirds. Peter, aged nine, does considerably less than that. In fact when his father asked to stay on at the beginning of the growing season, the landlord told him he didn't see how he could keep him on another year raising a crop on so many acres and living in such a good house, with his family so "no-account."

Tom has been to school part of three grades. The Negro school in his district runs four months "normally" (the white school runs six); but in the year 1932-33 it closed altogether, and since then it has been averaging less than three months. Besides, cotton-picking season in Alabama runs well into November, and after that it is often too cold to go to school without shoes. So from January on Tom and Peter have been taking turns in one pair.

The older brother did a little better. He was a "prosperity" child, and during several of the 1925-29 seasons he got the full four-months school term. By the time he was thirteen, however, he had stopped going altogether, having finished the fifth grade (twenty months of education for a lifetime of work) and being, in the view of the riding boss, "plenty big for a man's work and likely to get uppity soon if he don't quit school."

In picking cotton Tom is not so much "smarter" than some of the younger children. At age twelve he can keep going longer, of course, at the end of a twelve-hour day with the thermometer still close to 100 degrees, than he could when he was seven, but he can hardly pick faster. All the children pick with both hands, and by the end of the first season the lifetime rhythm of pluck, pluck, drop-in-the-bag is long since established. But now that Tom is taller he has to stoop so much, or move along on his knees, while the littlest fellows scramble by with ''hardly a bend to them.'' The cotton plants often grow shoulder-high, to be sure, but the cotton bolls on them grow nearly all the way to the ground; so, for all but a tiny child, this means ''stooping, stooping all day.'' But Tom can manage the big sack that he drags after him by a shoulder strap better now than when he was a little fellow. It grows so heavy dragging along after the smallest pickers all day that it nearly makes up for the ''bends'' of the older ones.

Chopping cotton is much harder and is done under greater pressure for time, for the growing season will not wait. The six- and seven-year-old children do not engage in this, but Tom has long since become experienced. He handles the heavy hoe with a ready swing, cutting out the superfluous plants with a steady chop, chop, from sunrise to dark.

The ordinary hand hoeing after this is easier (Tom began with that as a little fellow, next after the picking), but still it is heavier than picking. It too requires a stooping position all day long, and the weight of the hoe and the earth are not inconsiderable.

What is Tom—and what are all the hundreds of thousands of his fellows in the cotton belt of the South—getting for this investment of his childhood? An outlook for the future, a foundation for something better for him later on, an immediate financial return even in his own pocket for his present wretched and stultifying toil? On the contrary, Tom is not only burying his own childhood in this cotton patch, he is drawing in return not a dollar of pay, from year's end to year's end. The landlord's account simply chalks up so many acres cultivated against the family's debts for the coming year, and if Tom or his brothers did not work, their father would not get his farm for the next season. Tom's and his family's reward is that he continue shoeless and abominably fed, oppressed and half-illiterate from those first months in the fields when he was six until he shall be an old man. . . .

Many urban children also had to go to work during the Depression, but there they encountered problems with child-labor laws, police, and the increasingly present social workers. Again, what impact did working have on a child's education? On his health? Did it change his status in his family? How much money was usually involved? What kinds of work? What did premature employment imply for the child's future?

This section is from The Survey, *71 (February, 1935), 40-41. The* Survey *was a magazine for social workers, a group that grew in size and importance in the 1930s, as government welfare programs had to expand to care for the vast numbers of unemployed people. Gertrude Springer, the author of this piece, wrote a monthly column for* The Survey *advising social workers how to deal with new and unfamiliar problems.*

Two hours of music had lifted Miss Bailey into blissful forgetfulness of the hard facts of life. But as she went out of the concert hall into the winter night reality descended on her.

"Pencil, lady, buy a pencil and help the unemployed." He wasn't more than ten, with a cheerful voice and gamin smile. His plaid lumber-jacket was strangely familiar. Four dozen of them Miss Bailey had requisitioned from the clothing bureau. As sure as she stood there this was one of "our" children, and, impulse to the contrary, she supposed she had to do something about it. "Just a social worker's night out," she told herself.

The boy, as wary as a rabbit when she introduced herself as from "the relief," muttered something about, . . . "You can't put the cops on me." She didn't get his name, she didn't even try. But presently he walked along with her to the street-car, and agreed that it was pretty cold, and that it looked like snow. When she gave him her card and invited him to come to see her after school, she hadn't the least idea that she'd ever see him again.

Three days later, just at closing time a skeptical-faced secretary put her head in the door. "There's a kid out here who says you told him to come. He won't give his name. Shall I get rid of him?" Miss Bailey, with a dozen things to be done before dinner, wished to goodness she had let sleeping dogs lie,—and had him in. He was curious but it took a good while to get him to talk. He knew all about the relief, what day the "grocery-order lady" came, and how long it took to get shoes and everything. The trouble was with his mother. She wouldn't give him money for movies and she had a fit when he asked her for roller-skates though he was the fastest roller-skater in the block. She'd told him to go and find out how hard it was to get money. She bawled him out when he came in late—if she caught him. Sure he went to school, but the teacher bawled him out too, "Gosh, one day when I went to sleep in the arithmetic!" But business was pretty fair. The night of the snowstorm he made eighty-five cents but nights when the cops chased him he didn't make a nickel. He was saving for the roller-skates, but what with movies and hot-dogs and everything. . . .

Before he left Miss Bailey had his name and he had her promise not to tell his mother about his visit.

"And now what?" she asked herself as she jotted a memo for next morning. "They're Miss Tucker's case. She can see his teacher and she'll find out that he's dull and droopy in school. She may—and she may not—be able to persuade the mother that the boy must have more regular sleep if he is to get along in school, and that running the streets at night at his age is dangerous business. She may be able to find a settlement or boy's club where the child will find what he wants. And of course there's the law, there are ways to stop it. But apparently he is in no immediate danger and sharp conflict with the law at this stage might do him more harm than good. Surely if we can avoid that and make his parents more responsible toward him, it will be better for him in the long run. But of course what the child wants are the things it takes money to buy. The parents have no money and the child has found out how to get it for himself. I know he should not be peddling on the streets at night or any other time. To permit him to do it is contrary to every principle I own. Yet, I can see his side of it too, and I know if we stop him by strong-arm methods we may be good and sorry. And to think that not more than twenty cents a week is at stake, yet there's so little we can do about it."

Earning children, relief workers report, are a growing problem with their families, occasioning not only conflict within the family but conflict in the worker herself with her principles at swords points with hard reality. When the relief system dooms a family to grocery-order subsistence for months on end, when the adults can bring in no cash and a child can, it is not easy for the worker to see her duty clear.

"I've been a child-laborite all my life and I still am," says a supervisor in a small industrial city, "But in the face of some of these situations I've had to shut my eyes and park my principles. We have a case right now that I hope won't be held against me in Heaven. There are two children working, well grown and husky both of them, and bringing in enough so that we only supplement with a small grocery order. We suspected the children were under age but everyone concerned denied it stoutly. Then one day when ages were not under discussion the mother made the mistake of showing the visitor the family Bible with all the birth dates carefully entered. The record showed both children under legal age for working papers,—but the mother said the record was wrong.

"Now if we had been conscientious we would have checked with the school records and called in the attendance officer. But we haven't. We have made sure that the children's working conditions are tolerable, that they have a little share of their earnings for their personal use and we've shut our eyes to the principle involved. For this particular family—not all families mind you—it seems better to maintain the status quo in which the family has a considerable independence of action, than to upset the apple-cart and throw them 100 percent on relief with all the demoralization and resentment that that would involve. And if that's treason make the . . ."

The problems raised by under-age earning children are, however, comparatively infrequent compared with those raised by children of proper age whose earnings are absorbed by the family necessity. In the beginning of the present situation workers were often troubled by boys and girls who assumed too much responsibility for their families, and denied themselves the normal and necessary expressions of youth. But now, they say, there is another temper abroad in the land, a new concept of individual responsibility that causes many young people to refuse to shoulder burdens.

"Every relief worker who read Coral Brooke's Youth Engulfed in the January Survey knows a dozen Johns and Aprils," writes the director of a relief bureau in a western city, "Young people who say, in effect, 'I didn't make this mess and I won't carry the load. I've got my own life to live.' Sometimes a boy just ups and leaves home and refuses to talk about it. All we can do then is not to quarrel with him, to try to explain him to the family and to keep the door open for him should he want to come back. Sometimes we find at the bottom of his discontent perfectly reasonable complaints which can be straightened out. The average youngster under twenty will, we find, return home and carry his share of the load if he has any hope at all that the home can hold the security and freedom that he wants.

"We had a case last fall that I'm afraid was too good to be typical, but anyway we like to talk about it. His name was Henry. He was just past seventeen and the oldest of eight. Shortly after his father died a year or so ago the family came on relief. The mother was a good manager and they got along pretty well. When Henry got a job at $80 a month she was in the seventh heaven, sure that they could soon go off relief entirely. As it was we budgeted the $80, allowing, as is our policy, $12 a month to Henry for lunches, car fares and clothes, and adjusting the family allowance accordingly. The next thing we heard was that Henry had gone to live with a boy friend on the west side.

"It was three weeks before the case worker could get him to meet her for lunch and it took three lunches before he talked. He'd had to share his bedroom at home with two younger brothers who wore his neckties and smoked his cigarettes and never let him alone. He didn't like the old neighborhood. His friends lived on the west side and he knew a man there who would teach him boxing. Most of all he wanted to live with his chum who didn't wear his things. No, he didn't have anything against his mother, she was all right and had had a tough break. Maybe he'd go to see her but he wouldn't go back to live.

"A month later Henry phoned. He'd seen a house on the west side that was for rent very cheap. What would we think if he took it for Ma and the kids. He could swing the rent, and pay a little board and if the relief would go on helping. . . . We told him it sounded like a good idea, but that it would work only if his mother and the other children liked it.

"We didn't hear any more for two weeks. Then a very proud mother came in to tell us that 'my boy Henry' had moved the flock into a 'swell house with a bathroom', that he was paying board and that they could manage with less relief. The case worker went home with her and saw all the house except Henry's room which was firmly locked. In the basement was a punching-bag. 'And you should see the boys that come here at night. Such good times they have.' When we figured out the budget we found that with the rent and his board paid Henry had left himself just $14 a month, only $2 more than the original allowance.

Although the live-my-own life youngster is often extremely trying to the relief workers the more thoughtful among them see his independence as a healthier symptom than complete docility. The young person who without protest gives every cent he makes to his family presents symptoms of delayed maturity and poverty of spirit that hold poor augury for his future as a human being.

"We have a girl now that one of our case workers, who knows her mental hygiene, is all worked up over," says a supervisor in an eastern city. "She's just too noble.

"We have a general policy on exemptions from earnings before budgeting begins. If an unmarried child is the wage earner and the pay is less than $10 a week we deduct twenty cents a day for lunches, whether bought or carried, car fare as needed, and $1.50 for clothing and incidentals. The rest is figured as family income. If the pay is more than $10 a week one third is left free to the earner and the rest is budgeted. But this girl Eva doesn't accept anything as her right. She turns over her pay envelop intact to her father with a conscious virtue that makes you want to slap her. She's eighteen, the oldest of six and makes $11 a week. She's entitled to $2.75 of that to spend on herself. But she walks two miles to work, carries for lunch such scraps as she picks up and wears everybody's left overs. I'll bet she hasn't had a whole pair of stockings for six months. She's the little, unattractive one in a big, handsome, selfish family who give her no consideration whatever. Of course the reason for her attitude

is plain—she wants the approval of her family and gives them everything in an effort to gain it. And she has no chance at all.

"That case worker is simply losing sleep over Eva. She's been over
and over the budget with the family and with Eva. She's passed out
sound doctrine on personality development and pointed out horrible
examples of its lack. Everybody agrees with her, but nothing happens. She proposed at one stage that Eva live with a cousin, pay
board and send money home. But not Eva. Maybe a good two-fisted
suitor would bring Eva to—or perhaps if she lost her job. But Eva
has nothing to lose but her chains—and she loves them."

The children described below did not have to work in the cotton
fields or on the streets, but the Depression put its mark on their lives
nevertheless. Why do you think so many of these children feel
ashamed of their situation? What are their attitudes toward relief
payments? What is the role of money in their lives?

From Mirra Komarovsky, The Unemployed Man and His Family:
The Effect of Unemployment upon the Status of the Man in Fifty-
nine Families *(New York: Dryden Press, 1940), 126-27.*

The absence of social life is true of the adults in the family. It is
not true in the same degree of the children. Nevertheless, the depression has affected them also. The children, even the youngest, are
already so deeply conditioned to the adult valuations that they feel
humiliated by the family's plight. It is sad to observe the shadow of
humiliation under which the children live from day to day. This affects their relations with their playmates. Furthermore, lack of money affects social life in a more direct way. Their clothes are inade-
quate and they are unable to do things with their associates. The
following cases are cited in illustration:

One girl, 15 years old, conceals from her friends that the family is
on relief. She says that her father receives compensation (others say
that their father is on a pension and still others say that the family
had savings). The girl begs her father not to forget himself and men-

tion relief when her friends are around. The child is in constant fear that the relief investigator will drop in while her friends are visiting her. She would never accept any clothes from the E.R.A. [Emergency Relief Administration] for fear her friends would recognize the source.

The little Baldwin boy is only 9 years old, but he refused to wear a jacket obtained from the Red Cross. This little boy explains to his playmates that he has no money for the movies or for candy because his parents believe that those things are not good for children.

One child refused to go to Sunday school without a penny to put into the collection plate. The children in another family, although missing the radio very much, do not go to the house of their friends to listen to the radio because they don't like to remind their friends that they do not have one. When this family finally acquired a radio, the children, according to their mother, were jubilant, and ran around telling one friend after another that they, *too,* had a radio.

There were three or four reported cases in which being on relief was used as a term of insult in a play group.

A 12-year-old girl told the following story: There are two girls, twins, in her school. Once the twins got into a fight with some girls, and the girls told them, ''We know you're on relief,'' and the twins didn't go back to school for a long time afterwards. Another girl got into a fight with a playmate who accused her of being on relief. The girl retorted, ''You're a good one to talk. You curse, and your mother curses and drinks, and she came home last night at two o'clock in the morning.''

One girl, 15 years old, said that being on relief was the worst thing that ever happened in her life. The kids in school found out about it, and several of the mean ones made nasty remarks about it.

An 8-year-old child was asked by a group of playmates to go to a movie with them. The boy went in to ask his mother for money, but she didn't have a cent to give him. Ashamed to confess the truth, the boy returned and said, ''Mother doesn't want me to go to movies, but she gave me some money for candy instead.''

The adolescent children are, of course, still more depressed by the situation. Many of them conceal being on relief from their friends. Mary Kilpatrick said that she confessed to her best friend that she was on relief only after the girl came to her one day upset and crying because her family had to go on relief. To console her Mary told her that her own family was on relief.

The girl in the Holman family doesn't go out with boys because she would be ashamed to have them call for her. Their flat in the back of the house is so shabby that she is ashamed to invite even her girl friends there. Another girl does not invite her friends to her home because the family has no electric light.

Clothes are, of course, the main economic problem of the girls. The daughter of an unemployed automobile mechanic said that she was ashamed to go to school in the dress that she had worn every day for the whole winter. Not only the adolescent girls, but the younger ones also, have confessed that they stopped going to church because they did not have the proper clothes.

The economic problems of the boys were somewhat different. Few of them complained about the humiliation of shabby homes for, even if they went out with girls, the customary arrangement was for the boy to call at the girl's home. Furthermore, clothes did not play so much of a role. What they complained of was the lack of spending money.

II. GROWTH

The 1930s was an especially hard time to be young. Suddenly, in the land of opportunity, there were no opportunities. How did the young people described below adjust to that circumstance? What types of jobs could they get? What relationship did they have to their families? Did the Depression affect their love lives?

From Coral Brooke, [Assistant Supervisor, Cook County Bureau of Public Welfare, Chicago] "Youth Engulfed," The Survey, *71 (January 1935), 10-12.*

In 1930 we were strong in our belief that the emergency required that working boys and girls should give up their own plans, their nightschool classes, their savings for marriage and so on, while the family needed temporary support. But the emergency has become a permanency and these boys and girls are protesting against the hardship of supporting unemployed fathers, brothers, sisters and others living in the home, on wages insufficient for their own needs.

Letters from these young people and their families, and interviews with them reveal the poignancy of their situation.

In July of this year, George Morley, age 20, said to a caseworker:

I feel like I was falling down a long dark shaft that has no end. If you could tell me what is at the end of this it would give me courage to go on.

The next day he wrote:

Thanks very much for discussing my problems with me. I am hoping you did not take away with you a misconception of my attitude towards my family, for I am not in any way disloyal or unwilling to help. You see, it is only natural for every mature animal to wean himself from his parents on reaching maturity; and at some time there comes to every normal man the urge to marry and rear a family of his own, that is to say, I am not an economic unit of the family and should have the opportunity to work for my own living. Of course, I believe in helping my folks; I have done it on a part-time job while attending college, but such help is not really help but sharing the poverty. If the relief agency is going to hamper the progress of young people by forever tying them down to their parents, their own future families will be dependent upon society. It is both economically unfair and socially unjust to expect me to continue to support my family.

Demetra Pappas, age 21, has been engaged to be married for several years. She works at a soda fountain, earning $11.85 a week. She accepts her responsibility to contribute her wages to the family, but both she and her parents bitterly resent not only the continual delay of her marriage, pending reemployment of her father, but the fact that she cannot prepare for her marriage with household supplies and trousseau, as is the custom of her family and race.

Mary O'Rourke's marriage was sacrificed that she might meet the needs of her family. Mary is the oldest of six children. Her father died before she was old enough to work, but relief supplemented her mother's earnings. She left school after the eighth grade, found a job, and helped support the family for a year. Then she fell in love and married. Her husband's income was sufficient to support himself and his wife, and he objected to Mary's working, but her family needed her help, so she took a job against his wishes. Presently his business took him to another city. Mary was torn between the desire to go with him and to stay by her family. She stayed. After a year and a half she lost track of her husband, and three years have now passed since she heard from him. She is bitter and her frustration is reflected in her work and in her social relationships.

Many young people are confused when they find themselves the recipients of relief. Their education developed an abhorrence towards dependency. They are ambitious for advancement but are unable to plan their lives since they must contribute their earnings to the family income.

David Turner, a tall, thin, handsome lad, is one of thirteen. His father is a laborer, but all the children have been to high-school and several to college. David worked his way through his junior year at law school but has been forced to stop. He feels a definite responsibility towards his family but is shaken between his duty and his desire to live his own life. For two years he has kept an accurate account of relief given to his family, that he may repay it when he is able.

Floyd Jones, age 21, a junior medical student, has earned his education thus far by working as a life guard during the summer. The $300 thus earned carries him through the school year. He is willing to pay for his board and room at home, but not the amount requested of him by the public agency. His father says, "We'd rather starve than have Floyd give up his studies."

Catherine Tito, a charming girl with a remarkable mind, is bent on an education. She earns $30 a month, which, with a University scholarship, will see her through. Up to this time Catherine has contributed her wages to the support of the family, but she is determined that nothing shall interfere with her plan for her own future.

Parents who have always been economically secure and who believed that success depended upon individual effort, often accept adverse circumstances as defeat. They become seclusive; the children cannot have friends; their home life is restricted; normal living is impossible.

Five years ago John C was worth $50,000. Now the family is on relief, but neither he nor his wife will permit their children to mention it. They will not participate in community life, nor allow their children to do so lest former acquaintances should recognize them. The children, in their late teens and early twenties, are exceptionally active young people who require recreation and companionship. They are so disturbed that they break down whenever home life is mentioned.

Working boys and girls are leaving their homes to live elsewhere in the belief that their families will not suffer since in any case they receive only the minimum budget.

Frances Ferraci's letter speaks for itself:

> I am writing this letter pursuant to the conversation of this afternoon with my dad. I am at present a young self-reliant girl but still taking orders. Your budget plan if even presented to the Humane Society for Animals (let alone for people) would be done away with. I am doing enough (if not more than enough) for my family. I cannot do any more. For the past two years (since I was graduated from highschool at the age of 16) I have been working. Work which has not brought any relief to my parents nor myself due to the fact that my complete earnings are totally accounted for in the budget not even allowing me enough for expenses. Also for the past two years I have turned over to the family a sum of $300 received as compensation from an accident which nearly cost me my life. Now is the terminal. I cannot do any more than I am doing. I am leaving the place I call home due to the above mentioned circumstances.

James Scott tells us that should he get a job at $20 a week he would be no better off than he is now earning $10 because his earnings would still all be budgeted and his own wants overlooked. His letter expressed his hopelessness:

> There isn't any reason for me to stay home any longer. My parents find it impossible to keep our imitation home together because they lack sufficient food, clothes, rent and other necessities. Continual moving, eating according to statistics, and having empty rooms to bring my friends to is not my idea of home.
>
> My pay has decreased with NRA [National Recovery Administration] so I cannot pay $7 a week any more. If I cannot have advantages from staying home I believe it would be advisable for me to leave, which I intend to do, regardless of consequences, within this week. I am hoping for the best, but am prepared for the worst.

In order to circumvent the policy of requiring employed children to contribute their earnings to the family income, the children do not tell the truth about their wages and frequently are upheld by their parents.

The case worker was surprised when a letter from an employer stated that Martin Evans, aged 19, was earning $15 a month more than he had said. The boy's mother said that he had discussed the budget with her and felt that he could not contribute to his family as much as the relief agency requested. Unless he were allowed a liberal sum for clothing and amusement, he would, she said, follow the example of his father and leave home.

Philip Foster finally kept a long delayed appointment with the case worker:

"I am paying my family $9 a week board and room. I can't give any more."

"But you are earning almost twice that amount."

Yes, but I promised to pay the doctor, and I had to have a suit of clothes. I'm paying $2 a week on it. . . . I have to pay bills that way because I never earn enough to pay them all at once. . . . I am going to nightschool, and I want to get married in December and I've got to pay these bills so I can start life with a clean slate. . . . I used to give all my check to my mother, she came to the factory for it. The fellows razzed me and the boss objected to the fuss. Finally, I told mother that if she came once more I'd lose my job. Anyhow, I was tired of getting what was left over and I'm old enough to handle my own money. Mother doesn't like my girl—she never likes anything I do. I sleep in the kitchen.

Young people who cannot obtain what they believe are necessities from their earnings, go in debt or "take a chance."

Isadore Liss, age 21, whose father is dead, is employed as a photographer by one of the leading Chicago newspapers, at $65 a month. In order to pay back rent the family borrowed money on its furniture at a high rate of interest. Isadore is engaged to be married and is paying installments on an engagement ring as well as on his clothes. As a result the family is deeply involved in debt.

April has given her wages to her family ever since she began working. Now she writes:

You people refuse to give my mother any more help because I'm working. I'm 21 years old and do not have to turn my whole pay in to support the whole family. I pay board. You wouldn't give my father a job, but how do you expect my board to cover expenses for all of us. I've lived and walked so long in rags, that now I'm working I want some half-way decent clothes.

There are four small children here who need milk and clothes if you expect them to be healthy and go to school. If you would give my father a job we wouldn't want any relief—we said that time and time again. Other fathers are working, why not him. So don't expect me to support this whole bunch. Get him a job and we will be off the relief. Then I'll help all I can.

A few weeks later April was caught in a leading department store helping herself to certain clothing she craved.

When a boy or girl acts as provider in his father's place it reverses family relationships. Jane Ross, 22, thoroughly enjoys her role as provider. "I'm leaving home," said her father as he slumped into my office. "It's about the money—we can't go along Jane's way—she won't give me her money cause she earns it and wants to spend it. Anyhow, her ma likes her better'n she does me."

Sam Willard, age 20, has been experimenting with the dried fruits in the ration box, and because of his suggestions at the pie bakery where he works, has secured two raises. He says:

I certainly enjoy being bossy. Because I'm working I get the best things to eat, the best light to read by, the best bed to sleep in, and everyone has to do as I say.

On the other hand young people are discouraged because the burden of supporting their families denies them the ordinary pleasures and opportunities of youth.

Stella Munn says:

You see, Miss Lord, food isn't the only thing I'm worried about. I hoped that with my wages, I could buy a few things for the house and a few clothes. But now I realize I'm working for the grocer and the landlady and I'm thoroughly discouraged. I have two dresses to my back, for work and Sundays too. As for the house, the only good piece of furniture we have is the kitchen stove. I can't bring my friends to a house where they can't even sit down. All I'm asking for is a start so I can get things for the house, the children and myself. If my father had a job he could very well support us and I could buy the furniture. Why, we haven't had a rug on the floor for four years.

I don't think you would feel differently if you were in my shoes and had to work every day and sit at home and look at four walls every Saturday and Sunday and start all over again Monday. I haven't any girl friends because I can't dress the way they do. I can't go anywhere because I haven't any money. If I knew this existence was for only a short time I wouldn't feel this way, but it's been like this for over three years, ever since I started working, and we're worse off now than when I started.

I feel I've done all I can under the circumstances, and it's time something was done. I'm certainly old enough to know what I'm talking about, and I hope you can see things my way.

The King family consist of father, mother and three children. Mr. King has tuberculosis, and is unable to work. Annette, 21 years old, is employed by the American Medical Association, at $60 a month. She is concerned with the welfare of her family, and tries to do what she can, but her discouragement is deepening to resentment. She writes:

Below I will give you the list of things I bought for myself in the last two years:

1 pair of shoes	$2.50	
1 summer dress	1.00	
1 blouse	1.00	
1 hat	1.88	$6.38

Would you or any other girl of 21 like to live on this budget for two years? Wouldn't you like to be able to see a show with the girls you work with once in a while? So would I, but I can't.

All I get to wear is somebody's else old clothes. Would you like to go to work every day and not be able to buy a dress once in a while? I am only human, and I like nice things to wear the same as anybody else.

After the next month and a half, if my job lasts that long, I can get in line with the other unemployed. Won't even have car fare to look for work. You must know that when I went to work last summer we had bills stacked high—

Gas	$14.00	
Electricity	10.00	
Loans	35.00	$59.00

Who paid these bills? I did, by going without lunch. Now I have done all I can to help my family. But you people haven't been fair to me. And I am pretty discouraged.

For these young people there is, in our whole relief conception no plan except perhaps to save public money at their expense.

Have we the right to expect them to support their families, and, if so, how much longer shall we be able to exercise it? We are denying them the right to education, recreation and marriage, and to a normal chance to develop and maintain their capacity for complete living. They are bewildered, baffled, engulfed.

Shakespeare said that youth were to be found ". . . . creeping unwillingly to school." Does that describe American youth in the 1930s? What did education mean to them? Even if they could manage to complete their schooling, did it do them much good? What is the nature of the "generation gap" that Aubrey Williams (the head of the National Youth Administration) describes? What did the government try to do for young people in the Depression?

From Aubrey Williams, "A Crisis for Our Youth: A Task for the Nation," The New York Times Magazine, January 19, 1936.

A CRISIS FOR OUR YOUTH:
A TASK FOR THE NATION

by Aubrey Williams

It is natural to think of the unemployment problem as that of men and women who once had jobs and have now lost them. The bulk of unemployment is of that kind. The picture is not complete, however, unless we paint in the situation of the boys and girls who have reached working age since 1929 and who have not been employed at all or have been employed only intermittently and in dead-end occupations.

The fact is that there are an estimated 2,500,000 young people in America looking for work. Their numbers have been growing and must grow until society opens its ranks to make places for them. Pressing close behind them are the younger ones. In the three short years between 10 and 13, when a boy is still a child, his parents, his teachers, his pastor are hopeful about him and his chances in the outside world. They speak of what a fine boy he has become, of how well he has done in school, and either by word or implication lead him and themselves to believe that he will find his place, that society will put a value upon him, and that he will merit it and continue to merit it.

Soon he joins his older brothers, and realizes with them that there is no job for him. He has no money. He has no decent clothes. He finds other boys in the same plight as himself. By degrees he comes to the realization that he is outside the group that have things, that go places, that dress well, that somebody speaks well of, and that somebody finds valuable. He must have come from something, but as far as he can determine he is going nowhere.

That is the position of a large fraction of American youth today. It feels as if it had been very nearly pushed off the edge of the world. Break down the totals and the picture becomes even more appalling. Take the whole of our young people between the ages of 16 and 24.

More than one in seven are heads or members of relief families. Of the 600,000 who live in urban areas and are of school age 300,000 are not in school and are not working or seeking work. Considerably more than half have had some work experience, but three-fourths of these are unskilled or semi-skilled, and only 5 per cent of the whole unemployed group of young people consists of skilled workers.

Perhaps 60,000 have had some college education. At the other extreme 12,000 have had no formal schooling at all. Some 55,000 have broken loose from home ties.

About one-fourth, following the normal instinct of ambitious youth, have married. Almost 10 per cent are heads of families and a considerable proportion of these families have children. Thus there are wide variations within the general framework, yet the plight of all these young people is similar in that they are being denied a chance to make their way in the world during the very years when their enthusiasm, energy and desire to learn would make them highly useful to themselves and to society. The best of them should be in training to be leaders of their generation, the others to be capable followers. This great opportunity in human conservation is in danger of being lost.

How shall we avoid this calamity? What sort of treatment and assistance can be given to these innocent victims of a situation which they had no part in bringing about? If these youths had been well fed and housed in childhood, which most of them were not, they would now be at the peak of health and energy. Even so, they exhibit in every move, plan and instinct that these years, since they are their mating years, are in a sense their fiercest years. Fiercely competitive, fiercely ambitious. They want the best sweethearts, the best clothes, the best records in sports and social accomplishment that they will ever want.

They are, or should be, strong enough to mix concrete or run typewriters all day long, and still dance half the night. But they are haunted by desperate questions. Consciously, unconsciously, subconsciously, through every hour of their days, must run distracting uncertainties. What is to become of them? Can they marry? If marriage has already been achieved, how can they support their families?

It is not easy to be philosophical about this situation. It will not interest a young man who is hiding because he needs a haircut to be told that he is neither at the beginning nor the end of American history, that American youth has been crowded off the edge of cultivation repeatedly since the Colonies were settled, and that though geographical pioneering has ended it is still possible for the older members of the social group to move over and make room for the younger.

There still is plenty of work to do of a sort that youth can do best. Yet somehow we do have to convince millions of our young people that we have not yet come to a social domesday, and that there is something better for them to do than to jump off the deep end—a phrase common among them which apparently covers everything from lawlessness to resignation, despair and even suicide.

If we look back, the nature of previous solutions of this problem is plain to read. From the time when we ourselves were a frontier of Europe until 1890, when the Director of the Census ruled that this country had ceased to have a frontier line, the frontiers of American youth were physical frontiers. Going beyond the Alleghenies, past the Mississippi, past the Missouri where it runs north and south, westward to California in the Gold Rush, east again to the Great Plains, then to the woods of Northern Michigan, Wisconsin and Minnesota, American youth physically conquered the continent. Its electric connective to the future was the vitalizing alliance of new men with new ground.

Now we are forty-five years away from the last geographical frontier. Millions of men registered as children in the census of 1890 have been superannuated less by age than by newly invented machines. Up to 1890 a strong young man seeking his fortune could still find good and unplowed soil. It may have been less the lure of new lands than the thrust of restricted opportunities at home that sent him forth.

In most cases he probably was not a born explorer and adventurer—if we read the personal chronicles of the westward movement we find few Daniel Boones. But the land was there. Restless and penniless youth had an outlet. A little later, the new lands gone, the mountaineers were coming down from their eroded potato patches to dig in the mines for wages, and the sharecroppers were seeking in the factories a better lot than they could find in somebody else's fields.

From conquering land American energies were turned to the conquest of nature in other ways. In the very decade that marked the end of the historic frontier 208,000 patents were granted in the United

States. The velocity of invention was accelerated until in the decade ending in 1930, 421,000 patents were granted. This kind of pioneering made jobs, but it also pushed men out of jobs. For those who were pushed out, for the newer generations as they came of age, there were, with scant exceptions, no new homesteads.

The attitude of the nation toward the young had not changed. They were still expected to fend for themselves and the tradition that they would be well able to fend for themselves outlasted the conditions which had produced it.

The youths born in the years near 1890 did a job that has changed the face of the world and reconstructed the meaning of life. From them, essentially, came the automobile, the radio, the airplane, the improved and widely used telephone, the internal-combustion engine, the steel skyscraper, the linotype, together with the skill and knowledge to keep all this intricate apparatus running.

They taught us to send photographs by wireless, to cast a lens for mapping new universes; they enabled housewives to make ice in their kitchens, to build fires under the pot by turning a button; they released for nearly everyone chamber music once heard only in palaces and symphonies once heard only from the pits of orchestra halls; they telephoned across the ocean and flew around the world; they even lengthened the span of life.

Their achievements were not all positive. Sometimes they were stupid and neglectful of the rights of men and even of the expediencies which might have oiled the production machine which they were setting up. Their frontier manners were often more ruthless than any ever seen in a gun-toting mining camp.

The workers too frequently stood in line of the firing and went down in wind-rows before poverty and insecurity. In a sense the accomplishments of the generation of 1890 created the troubles facing the generation of 1936. Youth pushed itself out of its own country. It enclosed land against its own children. It grew two blades of grass where one had grown before, replaced hemlocks with peach trees and skunk cabbage with lettuce, opened up the ether as though it were a corner cupboard—then found suddenly that its estate was bankrupt.

So much, of good and bad, the youth of 1890 achieved. There is no reason to fear that the youth of 1936, if given a chance, cannot do at least as much that is good. There is reason to hope that the youth of 1936, if given help and guidance during these critical years, may avoid some of the mistakes made by its predecessors.

But guidance and help are needed. Our era is not totally different from that which preceded it, for eras do not abruptly close down over night. The world, which is at hand for the young to conquer, the world of economic rearrangement and readjustment, is neither new nor irrelevant to what has gone before. None the less, new elements have come into it.

Our production process, once a simple relationship of man, tools and materials, has now become a mass process, with masses of tools, worked upon by masses of men, to create masses of products. It can no longer be operated on the theory that the process of distributing the products must be individual, that, as an individual, a man can buy back what he makes.

Men grow rich, or merely comfortable, only because the collective forces are on their side. We can no longer ask wage-earners to fight poverty single-handed. We can no longer turn our young loose in the national pasture and expect them to grow fat. We cannot consider our youth problem as one of individuals, some of whom will be lucky, while others will fail. We must give all youth its chance, and to do this a certain amount of cooperative social action will be necessary.

The aims and possible accomplishments of the National Youth Administration must seem small and niggardly when placed against the canvas of this enormous task. We can do nothing but grubstake a few pioneers, tide them over, see that some of the same ones that start out over the high passes are the ones that reach the fertile valleys on the other side.

The Youth Administration can deal only with those among the young people who are in material need. It is doing something for them. So far it has succeeded in keeping in high schools and colleges approximately 300,000 students. More than 4,000 graduate students are being permitted to pursue their studies with NYA aid in 136 colleges and universities. Their stipend may not go over $30 a month and in most cases it is $25 a month, but it may make the difference between destructive idleness and training for a useful occupation.

For 100,000 undergraduates in nearly 1,600 colleges and universities there is a monthly allowance of $15, earned by a real contribution of work to research, library, museum or laboratory service, or to community projects off the campus. Finally, there are nearly 200,000 high school students, who receive only $6 a month—a small sum, but one which frequently makes the difference between school and no school.

In addition to these individual aids, steps are being taken to organize work of collegiate grade where no higher educational facilities exist, so that college work will be accessible to boys and girls who live at home. On our whole school program, small and thinly spread out though it is, since it touches only a tenth of the unemployed youth of the country, we are spending $27,000,000 out of our budget of $50,000,000.

Other young people are being helped through work on WPA projects or on NYA projects organized especially for and designed to fit into the needs of those between 16 and 24. The question of how many can receive such opportunities is primarily one of the amount of money available. We could find useful and necessary work far beyond the boundaries of the present limited program.

Beyond these main functions of our program we are undertaking a whole group of efforts designed to benefit young people directly and indirectly. The first of these is the furnishing of additional personnel to the United States Employment Service to help find jobs which are universally recognized as suitable for young people.

Needless to say, we are exercising extreme caution to make sure that cheap and unskilled young workers are not enlisted to force out older and better-paid workers at the top. We are financing the Federal Committee for Apprentice Training, set up a few years ago in the Department of Labor, and through that agency, approved both by organized labor and organized employers, shall try to place young people from both relief and non-relief families in apprentice jobs where they can learn regular trades. Apprentice wages are paid, of course, by the employer and not by the government.

In addition to this we are everywhere attempting to make available a large number of practical activities for young people who have nothing on their hands but time. In State after State the Youth Directors are activating agencies to organize latent goodwill and interest in underprivileged boys and girls. Churches, Y.M.C.A.'s and literally hundreds of associations for the young are cooperating. All are helping us to see to it that these youngsters shall be included as a living and functioning part of their communities.

Looking beyond the immediate task we can perform with $50,000,000 we see a vast field yet to be cultivated—a real national undertaking to conserve the morale and the as yet untested capabilities of the coming generation.

I believe that we must broaden our school system until we reach some arrangement whereby we can make education meet more nearly the needs of life. We have got to make clear that the services of farmers will never be used up in farming until every child has enough of the right sort of food to eat; that the services of industrial workers should always be in demand until we reach the place where the poor can be as warm in winter as wool and fuel can make them; that the services of economists and accountants, of clerks, salesmen, delivery boys, railroads, trucks and highways, of telephone and mail services, will never be over-employed until the necessaries reach every home; that the building trades, or the housing factories which may in part replace them, will never reach overcapacity until every family has a home of its own; that writers, painters and musicians are not too many or too prolific until they make available to all the expression of what life can mean.

This is a task which we may begin for youth but which must be carried on by youth. The urgent need in this crisis is that we shall not throw away or spoil our human resources, and particularly that we shall conserve the health and the enthusiasm of the young. Youth must rebuild what has been destroyed. It is the nation's most precious asset, now and in the years that are coming. We must not let a single spark of that splendid fire go out, in the boredom, hopelessness and actual want that unemployment brings to those who meet it at the threshold of their active lives.

One of the most popular programs that the government inaugurated during the Depression was the Civilian Conservation Corps. It took an "army" of more than two million young men into the woods and gave them employment, as well as a small income, most of which the government sent home to their families. Were there peculiarly

"American" aspects to this relief program? What effect did the CCC have on the American landscape? Was it a new experience for the young men who went to the camps? Other than conservation and relief, what other purposes did the camps serve?

From Frank Ernest Hill, "The CCC Marches Toward a New Destiny," The New York Times Magazine, February 21, 1937.

THE CCC MARCHES TOWARD A NEW DESTINY

by Frank Ernest Hill

As the Civilian Conservation Corps marches toward its fourth birthday next month it bids fair to achieve a secure place as a training school for American youth and a peacetime force for the husbandry of national resources. Director Robert Fechner, in a letter to President Roosevelt, definitely proposed such a rôle for it and the President has said that his governmental reorganization program includes a permanent CCC. Meanwhile, provision has been made for its continuance to June 30.

Millions of Americans have had glimpses of the stream of young men passing through the CCC camps—the total number is now mounting toward 2,000,000. They have on occasion seen these young men at work in the city, State and national parks; they have noted roads, bridges and recreation buildings constructed by them, have heard of their fighting floods and forest fires; planting trees and working on farms and watersheds to protect the soil from erosion. But they have not seen what goes on from hour to hour in the 2,084 camps of the "tree army" which dot the mountains, prairies or deserts of almost every American State; and it is here, perhaps, that one may discover what value lies in all this activity for the nation and its youth. Let us walk out into the shadowy air of morning as the bugle rouses the 200 men of a camp from their night's sleep and follow them through their day's work.

We are in the Georgia hills. An officer in uniform stands beside the bugler. The "enrollees" emerge from the low buildings half hidden among the pines and stand at attention as the flag runs to the top of the staff. There is a brief report on attendance, a word of dismissal, and the men saunter individually (never in military formation) to the mess hall for a breakfast of prunes, corn flakes, eggs, bacon and coffee.

They are boyish but rugged in appearance. Mostly from Georgia, and many from these very hills, they have the "Anglo-Saxon" look of most Southerners. Sun and brisk weather have tanned and ruddied their faces. In the kitchen, with its great range and serving tables and electric ice box (operated by the camp's own plant), a corps of enrolled cooks is busy, and enrolled waiters carry the food to separate tables where leaders survey its orderly distribution.

Outside, after breakfast, several trucks draw up near the administration building, in the center of the little flat among the trees where the camp lies. The men pile into them, pack them full, and stand holding one another and the side rails of the trucks. They wear caps with ear-flaps, mackinaws, heavy shoes—all government-issued. They stamp and whistle or chaff the enrolled drivers: "Step on it, Tom!" "Let's go!" And soon the trucks move off with a grinding of gears to the "work job" five miles distant.

Now the camp has emerged clearly in the morning light. Most of its dozen oblong buildings are on the flat; a few peer from the trees on the surrounding hills. They are of unpainted wood, but the door and window frames are touched with color. Whitewashed stones border the road that comes to an end in this remote work settlement.

Before the headquarters are the ghosts of garden plots that bloomed in summer. Walks paved with stones taken from the hills connect most of the structures: infirmary, recreation hall, officers' quarters, garage. The goal posts of a basketball court and the seats of a crude amphitheater set in the curve of a hill suggest some of the activities that occupy the men after their day's work. And there is a log schoolhouse built from the trees of the forest by the labor of the men.

Inside these buildings you will find wood-burning stoves for heat. In the washroom there are showers and tubs for laundry. The barracks show their two rows of army cots with chests at the foot of each for the men's belongings. An "overhead" detail of half a dozen men takes care of the buildings and grounds. Another detail taps typewriters and files papers in the camp office. It is a self-manned unit, this camp, simple and in some respects almost primitive, but neat and efficiently manned.

A short run by car takes one to the work job. Some of the men are doing forest improvement—clearing dead wood, thinning trees, running a trail. Another detail is completing a stone bridge. There is a variety of labor: some workers drive and man a truck bringing rocks; others swing picks and shovels; others are masons. A watchful foreman stands by, and occasionally a man comes to him for directions. Once he bends in brief consultation over a blueprint.

They will work here until noon, then into the trucks and back to the mess hall for a hot lunch, then to the job again until the eight-hour day closes in the late afternoon. Supper is over by 6 P.M. and there is a long evening ahead for talk or reading in the barracks (every camp has its library, often running to a thousand volumes), or ping pong or letter-writing or gossip at the counter of the post exchange, or work in one of the classes which make up the camp's education program.

This is a typical camp—so far as any is typical. In New York and New England the men are often of Italian, Irish, Polish and Jewish stock; there are more Germanic and Scandinavian contingents in the Middle West; there are French in Louisiana. And the buildings and grounds and facilities vary with the ambitions and energies of the army officers who administer, the forestry or park or soil erosion experts who guide the work, the camp adviser who presides over education, and the men themselves. But a common spirit pervades all the camps, and there is a certain common denominator of appearance and action.

These reflect the philosophy of the CCC officials as it has developed in more than three years of experience. In flavor this spirit is democratic. Those in charge of the camps and their work regard the men with whom they deal as fellow-Americans and individuals.

There is also a strong pioneer aspect to the CCC philosophy. The sites of the camps, nearly all in untamed parts of the land, almost necessitate this. So do the limitations of the CCC budget. "Making something out of nothing" is a problem with officials and men, but both have faced it with an almost joyous courage.

The astounding and almost elegant appointments of the best camps—recreation halls with hardwood floors, schoolhouses (not provided for in any budget), motion-picture projectors, museums, theaters, athletic fields—all are made possible by savings from the post exchange profits, by volunteer labor, or by "chiseling" on the good-will and pride of near-by communities. But the democratic and pioneer aspects of camp life are in turn part of an emphasized purpose to "rebuild" the young men who enter the CCC.

This purpose was not dominant at first: relief and work were the original objectives of the CCC. But President Roosevelt, its founder, early stressed the "moral and spiritual values" which lay potentially in the organization, and experience has made these of greater importance. These young men are jobless, often ill-educated, often without training, often physically below par. The corps has gradually widened and deepened and made more conscious its program for their rehabilitation.

Its specific goals are now (1) to build up the physical man by giving him clean, comfortable surroundings, good food and healthful work; (2) to develop work skills in all interested men as they labor at their daily tasks; (3) to discover by personal conference their abilities and inclinations; (4) to further these through the field work or through educational courses of a practical nature; (5) to give each man some sense of his duties and privileges as a citizen in American society, and (6) through all these processes to breed new confidence and a desire and capacity to go back to active work in home communities.

The educational program has formed a kind of center for CCC philosophy. The camp adviser holds individual conferences, ascertains "the needs and wishes of the men" in planning courses, and brings in the officers and park or forestry officials to further the general plan.

Men interested in the road building they do during the day will find their superintendent or foreman teaching masonry or surveying at night. Officers and technical staff members and teachers employed by State relief agencies, and the adviser and some of the qualified enrolled men give courses like automobile mechanics, business English, woodworking, American history, current events, tree identification, office practice and journalism.

The classes are informal groups, and the academic flavor is discouraged. They stick close to prospects for employment or conditions of life which the men may face when they leave camp. And their popularity is shown by the fact that, while going to "school" is voluntary except for illiterates (some 9,000 of whom yearly are taught to read and write), more than 60 per cent of the 323,000 men now in the corps are engaged in some kind of study.

What does all this activity mean to those who receive its benefits? One way of finding out is to ask the men. But the answer may be had more succinctly from one of the editors of Happy Days, the unofficial camp paper for the entire corps, who has probably observed more CCC camps and men than any other outsider. He made an estimate that from 15 to 25 per cent of the men are really "rebuilt."

"They find health, training, new knowledge, new ambition in the CCC," he said. "The great majority make definite but smaller gains. The rest get little"—besides the $30 a month each receives in addition to his board and lodging, of which about three-fourths goes to his family. This estimate tallies well with my own observations in more than one hundred camps in all parts of the country.

But CCC officials claim no more than that they stimulate many men, show them possibilities in themselves, give them preliminary training. The maximum of eighteen months is indeed too short to do more. However, they can point to foremen in the organization who were once enrolled men, and to the fact that from 25 to 40 per cent of the men get and keep jobs after leaving the corps.

Certain charges have been made against the CCC which are considered in weighing its benefits. The most important of these has been that the camps are a camouflaged military activity. The army administers the corps, but the officers in charge of camps function under severe orders to impose no military training on the men; and the army carries out orders. The army insists on standards, but enrolled men will walk up to a commandant with a "Say, Captain," as fearlessly as they would approach an employer or the principal of a school. And the officers have no control over the boys while the latter are at work. The park or forestry or soil erosion officials supervise the work jobs, and their influence is perhaps the dominant one in the camps.

Other criticisms run to the effect that the food is bad, that living quarters are poor, that officials are domineering or inert, and that there are restrictions upon freedom of speech. One or more of these may be true of individual camps at times, but except for the last all are essentially without foundation.

There is a real basis for the charge that free discussion of social and political matters is not permitted in many camps. Army officers fear "Communists" and "agitators" and zealously discourage them. Many of the educational staff protest; some camps boast that any radical may speak his mind freely. But in general he may not.

Consideration of the CCC involves not only the atmosphere of the camps and its effect on individuals but a look at the balance sheet of work done and expense involved. The figures are impressive in sheer size. About 1,900,000 men have passed through the corps since April, 1933, including the 350,000 now enrolled. They have accomplished much both in amount and variety. They have built, for example, more than 82,000 miles of truck trails and minor roads; planted 1,000,000,000 trees, constructed 3,000,000 check dams and treated 3,800,000 acres in soil-erosion control work. They have fought fires and engaged in many other activities.

The cost of the camps to Jan. 1 is estimated at a little more than $1,400,000,000; during the fiscal year ended last June 30 it was $492,000,000. Appropriations made by the last Congress were $308,000,000 from July 1, 1936 to March 31, 1937; and the deficiency bill signed recently by the President included an item of $95,000,000 for CCC work from April 1 to June 30.

Those who advocate the permanence of the corps set against the necessary outlay certain intangible but important social advantages.

It is, they point out, an institution peculiarly American in character—wholly different in spirit and practice from European experiments in work camps such as Hitler's labor battalions. And by its combination of work and study it has reached destitute and underprivileged boys as no other agency could. The bulk of these have been "through with school." But the CCC has found a way of carrying on where the schools could not, of converting relatively poor material into useful and sometimes very valuable material.

They argue also that not only the underprivileged will profit by such training as the camps give. Boys from various economic levels fail to make a right adjustment to life in the conventional surroundings. With such an approach to their problems as the CCC affords, many would find themselves.

Finally, they assert that the CCC has come at a time when the nation is in need of such a force for dealing with its public domain. The national and State parks and forests have increased in number; the forces that care for them are insufficient. Soil erosion has arisen as a new problem; here too is a service ground for youth. The nation will profit, they argue, by retaining the CCC, adjustable in size to economic emergency, as a means for saving its youth and its domain.

Undoubtedly the CCC has exerted a vitalizing force on the young men of America. It has taught many of them the meaning of work, something of citizenship, and pointed the way to the skill and knowledge which make citizenship more worth while. It has given many of them new health and new courage.

And no less has it contributed toward saving or improving the wilder part of the American land—mostly the property of the American public. The park and forestry services have been able to indicate what could be done with a force of young workers: valuable conservation work which they say could not otherwise have been accomplished in a quarter of a century. And they report today that there is an indefinite amount of important protective work still to be done.

The following selection gives special attention to the young college graduate of the 1930s. What are the criticisms the authors make of the C.C.C.? What differences do they note between the situations of young men and young women? What do they say about racial and religious discrimination in the job market? Were hard times harder for some people than for others? Why?

From George R. Leighton and Richard Hellman, "Half Slave, Half Free: Unemployment, the Depression, and American Young People," Harper's Magazine, 171 (August, 1935), 342-49.

In many respects the post-1929 college graduate is the American tragedy. He is all dressed up with no place to go. He finds himself trained, but without any chance to use his training. One sample here will suffice. There were 50,000 young men studying engineering in

1920; 75,000 in 1930. "Electrical engineering led the increase," says Dr. E. B. Roberts of the Westinghouse Electric and Manufacturing Company. "All this was in response to . . . the loud voice of industry demanding more and more technically trained men. If ever an educational system made an effort to adjust itself to the demands thrown upon it, it was our engineering schools." To what end? At the moment there are more than 50,000 unemployed engineers.

The number of male college graduates for the five years of 1929-1934 was between 1-1/2 and 2 millions. During these years college appointment offices have generally placed the percentage of unemployment between 50 and 85 per cent. The actual figures, however, are appreciably higher. A considerable percentage of the 1929-32 graduates who were employed at graduation have since lost their positions. Moreover, a large part of the graduating classes goes on to the professional and graduate schools and, therefore, is not to be included in the base on which the percentage of unemployed is computed.

Now what happens to these young people? Let us suppose that in 1926, at the age of 22, a young man graduated from college and got a position. This left him until 1929, three years of slow, conservative, and uneventful development toward a permanent place in his occupation. After this brief period, which finds him still in the formative stage of his wage-earning career, he loses his job. For many reasons, he is less favorably situated now than at 22. For at 22 his habits were potentially susceptible to direction along the lines of many different occupations. At 25 the fact that he has already worked at one particular calling would make him undesirable from the point of many employers in other kinds of business.

There follows a period of five years of practically complete unemployment. Occasionally he may secure temporary employment at a salary of fifteen dollars a week or less, in what is often a distasteful job that no one else wants. Of hope for the future there is little. Should economic conditions return to the most prosperous level of 1929, his chances of reëmployment are still very uncertain.

The vicissitudes through which this young man and his fellows may pass are sometimes illuminating to the observer if not to the young man. One such, the son of an executive in a large business, graduated from college three years ago and, despite the efforts of his father, has as yet been unable to get a job. Now observe the father. A few weeks ago the father called an employment agency on the telephone. He needed a stenographer who must be male, must have graduated from high school not earlier than 1934, could not be older than eighteen; he must be white, Protestant, and the "American type"; he must be ambitious, aggressive, and accustomed to dealing with people. The pay was fifteen dollars a week, attendance at evening sessions of a local college would be encouraged, and there were opportunities for promotion.

We need not pause for acid comment on the white, Protestant, and "American type" requirements. But the other demands require some translation. There are thousands of competent girl stenographers looking for jobs. Why is a boy asked for? Because the job of a male stenographer can be expanded by degrees into that of a semi-executive and that is where his ambition, aggressiveness, and skill in dealing with people will come in. But he is hired as a stenographer and such he may, in theory, remain and with a great saving in pay. Why must he have graduated from high school no earlier than 1934? There are thousands of boys who have graduated from high school—and college—since 1929 and whose jobs, if any, have been temporary. Business doesn't want them. They're "rusty," they've got into "idle habits," they're "undependable." It's the youngest who are wanted and wanted cheap. But all this while the son of the executive who is doing this hiring is without a job and is himself in the crowd that his father won't touch. The father begs the employment agency to find his son a job elsewhere—where the same attitude is present!

This paradox is repeated with variations. We have trained young people—including those with a technical high-school education that prepares for apprenticeships and college and professional school graduates who hold degrees in medicine or engineering or a dozen other fields. These young people are trained, but they have no experience. If a job calls for experience, the man who has it will probably be someone who was out of school and employed before 1929. If no experience is necessary, the employer will probably fill the job with the youngest, fresh from school. Those who fall in the years between are lost.

A young man out of medical school in '31 and still looking for an internship has far less chance of getting it than the man who graduates in '35, and it is going to be very difficult for the '35 man with the best of luck. If perchance the graduate is a Jew or a Negro he might as well declare his medical career at an end right now. He was through—forever—before he had a chance to start. And all this despite the fact that there are nowhere near enough doctors to look after our 127,000,000 odd people.

The report of an investigation of unemployment among young people in England makes an admirable statement of the case there which describes our own quite as accurately:

> . . . in the distributive trades large numbers of children, particularly boys, are willing to take employment, because of the absence of other occupation, in the most menial tasks which cannot fit them in any way for a life of useful work. The community is taking advantage of the plight of juveniles to make them hewers of wood and drawers of water for a time until they can be replaced in the same work by a new flood of children direct from school. . . . Finally the depression has produced the paradox that the children who have had the longest training seem least able to obtain employment.

The position of the C.C.C. camps deserves scrutiny, especially since it is argued insistently that the enterprise become an established part of the national policy. Quite aside from food strikes, camp revolts, the discharge of boys for "communistic and bolshevistic plots," the urging of more military training by the Chief of Staff, and other sour episodes which have spotted the history of the C.C.C., there is the vital question of what these camps are supposed to accomplish. Often they have saved boys from destitution and demoralization and have served as a means of physical rehabilitation. But rehabilitation for what? A return to a world where jobs are just as few as they were before? A permanent establishment implies acknowledgment of a permanent state of unemployment. In what way can the camps be regarded as a "solution"? When their period of enrollment expires the boys must go back to the same vicious half slave, half free environment from which they came. Any advantage which has been gained from forest experience must frequently be vitiated—especially in the case of town and city boys—by a newly created conflict between the old and new ways of living.

"The more military training a boy gets, the better employers like it," the authors were told in one instance. The reader may draw from this what conclusions he wishes. Other employers, bilious over the New Deal and all its works, may hesitate to employ boys who have spent time in camps, believing that the C.C.C. means just more vitiating made work. In either way, it's a case of cold storage, and after cold storage, what? Like eggs, a boy will not keep indefinitely.

Confidence in the educational side of the camps has been cracked by the suppression of Professor Ogburn's camp textbook and by the subsequent resignation of Dr. Marsh, the educational director. "There has been a 33 1/3 per cent turnover in camp educational advisers. As late as last February 430 camps were still without an adviser serving full time," says a recent article in the *New Republic*. The reader must remember that educational advisers are in a strictly subordinate position under the military camp commanders. "It is not the fault of the officers," says an article officially released by the Emergency Conservation Corps, ". . . if they tend to confuse a work camp with a private training course for themselves and an opportunity for building up a beautiful efficiency record for future use. The army judges results in a C.C.C. camp as it would judge results in an army or militia camp."

Great claims are made of the value of educational projects in the camps. But educational work is done at night after a day's work. A boy may come in to face a condition like this: "There was one schoolroom of moderate size with three tables that might seat ten students. There were no books; the entire equipment for the department cost $58. The library and ping-pong table were in the same room. The director said that 61 per cent of the men had enrolled and about 50 per cent of them were attending. Outside the nature study and forestry, the courses were not popular and did not seem appropriate." The sharing in the responsibility for the camps between the War Department and Mr. Robert Fechner, the Director of the C.C.C., leaves small room for confidence in the camps as a permanent enterprise. Mr. Fechner is an old-line labor-union organizer, and his conduct in the Ogburn case only deepens the profound doubt felt in the social courage and economic intelligence of our labor union bureaucracy.

"Most people who have had anything to do with the C.C.C. wish it to be made permanent and talk of William James's moral equivalent of war,'' says the *New Republic* article just referred to. ''Nevertheless, democratic institutions are probably best preserved when adolescent males remain within the family system and plan for families of their own. Camps might perhaps be continued by the government for boys who wish to make forestry a career. With this exception, the less this country does to prolong the gang age in its youth; the better.'' But it's being done, all the same, and the quota has just been doubled.

In the United States the tradition of working is extremely strong. Self-respect requires regular occupation. We have a leisure class, but they have never, like their European fellows, been accepted as a part of things. To make a million dollars has been a national passion; but self-made men have cursed any idleness in their own children, and the idle rich have long been taken as a butt of derision, contempt, and hatred by most Americans. To be sure, what a man worked at was less important than the fact that he worked; an industrious bucket-shop operator was more virtuous than an idle Vanderbilt.

We still call upon independence, initiative, and individual effort as our most sterling virtues. For all the discussion about the new leisure, our spiritual and material lives are still dominated by economic necessity. A job is needed even to enable a person to enjoy leisure. Under our civilization, these virtues cannot be realized except by people who possess the economic means to realize them.

> Divorced from the feudal and theological heritage (of Europe) [says Charles Beard], American life has been in the main hard, economic and realistic—a conquest of material things, and American thought has been essentially empirical, not metaphysical and theological. It is largely for this reason that European visitors, with their feudal and theological hangovers, have been almost unanimous in calling Americans ''money grubbers.'' To have food, clothing, shelter, comforts, and conveniences has been an essential preoccupation of Americans. The outstanding positive characteristic of American civilization, then, is preoccupation with economy in practice and empiricism and humanism in thought. Mass production, engineering and gigantic organization have been the outward manifestations of this primary American interest.

When a young man, born and bred in a country with this tradition, cannot find employment, the energy which he would normally expend through participation in the processes of production finds no outlet. He stagnates. His tissues weaken with forced passivity. His morale sags. And his determination becomes increasingly flaccid. Decadence of morale strikes him at the moment when he is beginning the most essential process of his adult life, earning a living. There is no job! The future, at a stroke, is cut off. There is small virtue in damning a young man who, after a year of hopeless salesman-on-commission jobs, thankfully took an imitation relief job. "I get eighteen a week, and I'm eighteen a week better off than I was before."

Examine the young men who find occupation as investigators or in some other capacity in relief administration. Here their wages are fixed—and low. There is practically no prospect of advancement. (Why don't you go down on your knees and thank God you've got a meal ticket? Why?) Their jobs, such as they are, are at the mercy of political forays and the jealous brawling between professional social workers and the political fraternity. Compassed about with such influences, the relief employee covers up. He does not have the protection which the civil service can occasionally extend. If he and his fellows attempt to organize for protection the red scare is raised. Low pay, insecurity, and espionage are his lot, and it is not surprising that he develops a poker face and a profound distrust of the stranger. For the sake of safety he won't—he can't—open his mouth. Whether on relief or off, the lost generation are hemmed in. A bound has been set that they may not pass over.

Much has been said and written about career women who are not interested in marriage. By far the majority of women, however, see marriage as a major business. If the man is not in a position, financially, to marry, both are involved in serious social, physiological, and spiritual maladjustments. Although the woman may be employed, marriage is difficult if the man is not, because such a position is repugnant to the average American.

From 19 to 29 is the marrying age. Marriage in many cases has been made possible by aid from the family: by living off the in-laws, by doubling up with them to save rents; by living on the wife's income as a temporary expedient; and even by going on government relief. Those who take the latter course at once find themselves a target for brickbats. "The government is supporting and allowing these people to breed in idleness." Further, at the moment of writing, the allowance for food for one person is 6.97 cents per meal in New York City where the nation's highest relief allowances prevail.

Nevertheless, the drop in marriages has been precipitous. Expressed in marriages per thousand of population, the fall has been even greater. For the first time since 1911 the number of marriages fell below the million mark in 1932. Yet the population in 1911 was 93 millions; in 1932 it was 125 millions, or over 34 per cent greater.

The story of economic enervation, as told in marriages, is repeated in the success of the C.C.C. in filling its ranks. This result has turned upon one factor: the economic helplessness of the lost generation. Despite the fact that 90 per cent of the enrolment is narrowly confined to the ages of 18 to 25, the full quota has always been assembled quickly and easily. In view of the very strong affinity between the sexes at this age, it must be very dire circumstances indeed which will send the young man off to the backwoods. "Boys do not come into the C.C.C. unless they are jobless, unmarried, and members of families on relief," says Jonathan Mitchell. "They know well enough that the normal course for young men of their age would be to find jobs in their native towns, take girls to the movies and plan on getting married and founding homes." For at least some of the boys, their own predicament and that of their families is the cause of intense worry. In a recent issue of the national C.C.C. newspaper, *Happy Days,* there is a naive story of a fictional C.C.C. boy who performs prodigies of wit and audacity to win a girl in the neighboring village, only to find she is about to marry a non-C.C.C. boy who has a job. A few weeks ago, in Camp 222 in Middleburg, New York, a debate was held before a tense audience on: "Can a Man Support a Wife on $25 a Week?" It would appear useless to labor the obvious farther.

From the time he leaves school the young man of the lost generation finds that his world goes into reverse. First he gets no job. Economically debilitated, he can neither sustain his spirit of independence nor express his initiative. Then the Devil begins to wreak his evil. The young man undergoes a profound spiritual metamorphosis. For underlying the need of a position, of the desire to marry and to establish a home, are powerful and fundamental forces. Their abuse may cause serious disturbances to the physical and mental health of the individual.

Most important of these forces is the need of sexual expression. Theoretically it may remain latent; our habits of life, however, stimulate it to a recurrent state of activity. Closely related is the powerful desire of two persons to live under a common roof. The only socially legitimate course of sexual expression is under the protection of marriage. If this course is denied there is a probability of increasing sexual illegitimacy, and in the absence of the latter, a serious neurotic unbalance.

There is also the desire to establish a normal family life. For most people the spiritual bases of the family are necessary. The stabilizing effect of family life, the mutual stimulation of personalities, mutual support in moments of stress, and a normal participation in community activity: without marriage these are lost.

III. LOVE AND MARRIAGE

For men who had prided themselves on their ability to provide for their families, going on relief was a difficult, trying experience. What did that experience do to men's self-esteem? How did it affect the attitudes of wives and children toward husbands and fathers? What other changes in family relationships did unemployment bring?

From Eli Ginzberg, The Unemployed *(New York: Harper and Brothers, 1943), 76-79.*

The work which men do around the house helps their morale and also eases their wives' burden. Some women, able to handle their own work, deliberately encouraged their husbands to help them, because they thought the men would be better off for having something to do. But working around the house was not all profit to the unemployed man. By taking on feminine duties he widened the breach between his old life and the new. His failure was underlined by this transgression of sex boundaries. Some men took so easily to their new work that one must suspect that it fulfilled an inner need. The better adjusted the unemployed man became, the more difficulties he had fighting his way back into private employment.

Many women were distressed by their husbands' failure to provide for the family. They had taken it for granted even prior to marriage that a husband would provide for his wife and children. When a man failed to carry out his obligations, his wife frequently lost her balance.

The most telling evidence is found in the changed attitude of many women toward intercourse. Mrs. Berkowitz said "that she had always hated 'it' but never felt that she could do anything about it. But now, 'thank God,' it was possible for her to sleep apart from her husband." Mrs. Wolf, a much younger woman, was even more outspoken. "She said that she had always been a cold person, little interested in sexual matters. When her husband was working and supporting her, she supposed it was his right to have sexual relations and she therefore acquiesced. Now she avoids it. She has limited sexual relations to once a week, and even tries to get out of this. She has not gone to the birth control clinic because she saw no reason for going through an examination and using contraceptives just to give her husband pleasure."

The excessive demands of Mr. Cohen had long been cause for friction, but Mrs. Cohen said that "as long as he made a living, they went along from day to day. Now it was impossible." In his office interview, Mr. Cohen plaintively remarked "that his wife is now 'wearing the pants' and this makes for disturbance in the family. He said that not even in Italy or Germany, where all sorts of queer things are happening, did the man fail to remain the head of the household. He realized that his wife had reason for complaint, now that he was no longer earning money. She keeps repeating 'F.D.R. is the head of the household since he gives me the money.' "

Even in families free of marital tension, the failure of the man to continue as breadwinner led to a shifting in authority, usually to his wife, occasionally to an older child. Mr. Jacobowitz knows "that his wife has lost all respect for him. She keeps nagging and annoying him for not being able to do better, but makes no helpful suggestions." Mrs. Jacobowitz is aware that when she is very much discouraged she scolds and nags him, but she tries to make up for it afterward. However, she feels sure that "the mother must be the backbone of the family." Conditions have changed in the Jaffe family. "Mr. Jaffe is no longer the man he once was. He was proud, confident, and admired. His wife looked up to him and was happy with him. She did her job in the home, and he out of it. They had many friends. Now they seem to be crawling around in a hole which seems to be closing over them. She is cross, scolds, and nags. She tries to stop, but cannot."

No family on Relief escaped without some heightening in tension, but most men and women tried hard to keep the tension within bounds. The Davidowitzes said "that they know how each suffers, and they do all that is possible to understand and help each other." Mrs. Finkelstein believes that not only "have family ties not suffered during unemployment, but, if anything, they have been strengthened 'since they all recognized that there was a need to work together and make a go of a very difficult situation.' "

When women understood that the men were not personally responsible for the family's plight, but were victims of circumstance, they had little reason to nag and scold. But they did not always understand, at least not at first. Mrs. Finnan remarked that "she had not realized that her husband had been caught in a widespread economic disaster, and at first had believed that he failed to put forth the effort necessary to support the family. She had even gone so far as to leave him temporarily. She quickly realized, however, that she had been very unjust and came back, and spent the remainder of the time trying to encourage him and helping him to keep up his spirits." Few wives went so far as Mrs. Finnan, but many went through the same cycle of accusation and understanding.

Despite the genuine efforts of many wives to support their husbands emotionally, the man's status deteriorated, especially in households with adolescent children. The fact that their fathers were not working, the fact that they were around the house all day, the fact that their mothers had to budget every penny—all these things proved their fathers were failures.

Many men were particularly sensitive about their failure to provide adequately for their children. Mrs. Atkinson said that her husband is most concerned about his inability to give his young daughter the things she really needs and wants. Her daughter, however, is very understanding and has never alluded to her deprivations. The Brills have a less understanding daughter. She wants things that other girls have and does not understand why she cannot have them. She does not see why her father cannot get a job like other men, and she tells him so. Mr. Brown related "that it makes him feel badly that his children have so little. It hurts him particularly because his daughter lets him know how little she has in comparison with other children." In the Gallagher family, things have reached an even worse impasse.

"According to both parents, the older children are unhappy because they want things they cannot have, and refuse to listen to reason when their father tries to explain why they cannot have certain things. They point to other fathers. This leads to much quarreling, for Mr. Gallagher has no patience with them because they are so unreasonable. When they make noise or annoy him, he flies off the handle."

Younger children were frequently unaware of being deprived, and many older children, sympathizing with their father's plight, spared him. Occasionally, as in the Solomon family, the father was able to give the children something other than money. "He has always taken an interest in the children and allowed them to monopolize as much of his time as they wished. Although he has had no schooling in this country, he is able to help them with their homework, and they are particularly proud of his mathematical ability."

Although few children went to the extreme of Mr. O'Brien's daughter, who said "that she does not believe her father is the person to criticize her because he doesn't have a real job himself," they observed that unemployment had deposed their father as head of the household and turned him into just another member of the family.

Often, as fathers lost their jobs and children were forced to find employment, a dramatic reversal of the usual family economic pattern took place. Now, instead of working parents and dependent children, many families came to be constituted of unemployed parents living on their sons' and daughters' wages. What psychological effects did this situation produce? What does the case described here suggest about the relationship between money and authority in our society?

From Mirra Komarovsky, The Unemployed Man and His Family: The Effect of Unemployment upon the Status of the Man in Fifty-nine Families *(New York: Dryden Press, 1940), 97-101.*

The Unemployed Father and His Working Child. The Brady case illustrates the relation between the unemployed father and the employed son. The decisive feature in the loss of the father's authority is the failure of the man as a provider, together with the gainful employment of the boy.

The Brady Family

Mr. Brady 46	Boy 22	Girl 15
Mrs. Brady 44	Boy 17	Boy 12
On relief since 1932.		

The boy of seventeen is the only employed member of the family, earning $12 a week.

Mr. Brady is a tall, well-built man with pure white hair combed straight back from a high forehead. He spoke well and concisely in the manner of a man who has arrived at a definite philosophy of life and who wishes to impart it to others.

Mr. Brady was a railroad engineer, earning a good deal of money and living well. He admitted that he used to be unfaithful to his wife. He went out with all kinds of women and drank rather heavily, but his wife was very "sweet" about it, and there were no major conflicts. He always saw to it that she and the children were well provided for. He used to have a violent temper. He left many a job simply because he got into an argument with the boss.

Soon after the family went on relief, Mr. Brady got interested in the Pentecost mission, better known by the name of "Holy Rollers." Mrs. Brady has always been very religious. Both of them were "saved" three years ago, and ever since that time they have taken a deep interest in the mission. They attend services, and Mr. Brady is one of the most prominent members of the mission.

Since Mr. Brady's conversion, marital life has been more satisfactory. He doesn't lose his temper as often. Mrs. Brady feels that life with her husband is much happier, and she gives thanks for her husband's salvation. His religious conversion and improvement in his temper apparently fully compensate her for economic hardships. Mr. Brady said, in fact, that his wife's respect for him has grown during the past three years. He has ceased looking for work and spends the day at the mission or reading the Bible or literature on the Bible or talking about politics. He is convinced that Communism, with the exception of its attitude towards the church, is the best political philosophy.

As to the children's reactions to the depression, Mr. Brady says that poorer clothing and being on relief have hit the children hardest. The 15-year-old-girl quit high school because of runs in her stockings, torn shoes, and worn-out dresses that she had to wear.

Mr. Brady says that while the children don't blame him for his unemployment, he is sure that they don't think as much about the old man as they used to. "It's only natural. When a father cannot support his family, supply them with clothing and good food, the children are bound to lose respect." If he had been earning, for example, he would not have allowed his son, 22, to quit school.

"It's perfectly true," he said, "that my word is not law around here as it once was." Mr. Brady felt that this was due in part to the fact that the children were getting older, but he feels also that his unemployment must have a lot to do with it, in addition. "When they see me hanging around the house all the time and know that I can't find work, it has its effect all right. I guess the children never expect to see me work again."

His unemployment has made the children feel independent. His working son, 17, seemed to have become old overnight. "The son of twenty-two is just like a father around the house. He tries to settle any little brother-and-sister fights and even encourages me and my wife."

Mr. Brady spoke of changes in the attitude of the children without bitterness, assuring the interviewer that they were good children, and that it was only natural for children to lose respect for an unemployed father. It appears that Mr. Brady finds his religion and prestige in the mission a balm for the loss of status with the children.

Mrs. Brady said that the burden of bringing up the children has always been hers. Mr. Brady had a very vicious temper and "whipped terribly hard." Since being "saved," Mr. Brady has become gentler and sweeter. Now the threat of whipping usually suffices because the children know he whips very hard, but he doesn't bother much with disciplining.

Mrs. Brady was somewhat evasive in her interview and did not admit any loss of respect on the part of the children. "Of course," she said, "the 17-year-old son is working and must be given more consideration. Everyone gets discouraged and irritable and sometimes the children get snappy. If we egged them on, there would be no end of arguments. We just keep quiet."

The best information on changes came from the children themselves. John, 22, impressed the interviewer as an easygoing, pleasant but lazy young man. He has looked for work but has not been able to find anything worth taking. He might find a job for $7.00, but "Hell, working all week for $7.00! There's no percentage in that."

John says that his father certainly lost control of the children. When his father was working—"when he was in the dough, his word was law. If you didn't like it, you got a sock in the jaw." If he had talked to his father four years ago the way Henry, the 17-year-old brother, talks to him now, his father would have "killed him."

When John was sixteen, he was helping his father repair a car. "Oh, you don't know any more about this than I do," he said. His father flung a hammer at him which laid him out. His father wouldn't dare to pull that now with his working brother. What's more, he wouldn't want to. "He is too discouraged and doesn't give a damn like he used to."

John told another incident. The father and two sons were working on the car. The father asked Henry to get a tool from the kitchen. "What do you think I am, your flunky?" answered Henry. He was not punished. At another time Henry was going out to see his girl. His father said, "Why don't you stay at home—it costs too much to go out so often." Henry said, "It's none of your business how much money I spend. It's mine. You keep your nose out of it." And his father was silent.

Only once in a great while does his father's old temper return. A couple of months ago Henry came from work in a bad humor and started cussing at the dinner table. His father told him to shut up. Henry mumbled something to the effect that his father should "go to the Devil." His father jumped out of his chair and went for Henry with his fists. But such things happen very seldom. In a couple of hours he was good-natured again.

Sometimes when the father says "Good morning," Henry might

answer "Go on—don't bother me." Henry has more to say than anyone else as to the expenditure of money. John says the change is very noticeable, because before the depression his father was the big boss. Now, if they get to arguing about money, Henry tells his father to bring in some money if he wants to kick so much.

Again, at times they have arguments over the food. Their mother might buy something for supper which their father didn't like; frankfurters, for example. His father would kick about it and feel that he was being discriminated against. "But money is the boss around here." Henry does more for the family than anyone else, so they cannot go against his wishes too much.

John summarized his attitude by saying, "I don't know that I have lost respect for the old man the way Henry has. I guess I sort of pity him. I feel like I want to help him. I'll tell you how it is. I feel he is more my equal than he used to be."

Henry is tall and thin. He appeared sulky and ill-humored to the interviewer. "The old man was right handy with his fists," he said, in describing his childhood. "I guess I got more than my share of what was coming to me. He used to get mad at me all the time. Whenever he said something, he wanted it done right away. If you didn't do it, he'd go for you. He was a pretty good father, I guess. He was very liberal with the kids and cheerful. He'd give you the shirt off his back, but we sure got plenty of lickings. He has calmed down a lot since he started going to the Pentecost mission. Besides, I'm my own boss now. Nobody can tell me what to do or how to spend my money. Working makes you feel independent. I remind them who makes the money. They don't say much. They just take it, that's all. *I'm* not the one on relief. I can't help feeling that way."

Henry said that seeing his father so discouraged and without ambition made him lose respect for him. "He is not the same father, that's all. You can't help not looking up to him like we used to. None of us is afraid of him like we used to be. That's natural, isn't it?"

The interviewer witnessed the following incident:

A peddler came and asked Mr. Brady for 8 cents for a head of cabbage that Mrs. Brady had bought. Henry tossed the peddler a dime. The peddler handed him 2 cents change, but Henry, indicating his father with a toss of his head, said, "Give them to him." Mr. Brady took the 2 cents silently.

Another incident occurred when the family was sitting around the dinner table. The family was almost finished with dinner when Henry came in. Mr. Brady got up immediately and surrendered his place at the table to him. There was no extra chair. Henry took the place at the table as a matter of fact without thanking his father for it.

The reaction of the two sons differed, but in both cases we witness change in attitudes towards the father as loss of respect and loss of fear. Furthermore, we observe complete loss of control over the children. Not only is the father helpless with regard to his sons' activities (his sons' going out too often and staying out too late, etc.), but he must meekly accept indignities, particularly from his working son.

The Robinson and Dorrance families tell very much the same story.

It is interesting to note that in families in which the role of the provider is taken over by one of the children the parents themselves often attempt to protect the authority of the working child. The parents are apparently afraid that if the wage-earning son is not treated well he might leave the family, thus withdrawing his support.

The Robinson boy, 17 years old, testified as follows:

"One thing," said he quite spontaneously, "we three younger kids were told to be nice to John and Edward. We were not supposed to argue with them at all because they were bringing in the dough."

The Brady family just described illustrates the same situation. The interview with the mother, the father, and the son revealed the indulgence of the parents towards the working son. The daughter said in her interview, "Henry thinks he is the king all right, supporting the family and all that, and the folks humor him along."

The Great Depression was the product of a general economic collapse, far beyond the control of any man or group of men. Yet individuals often blamed themselves for their predicament. They felt personal shame, guilt, and humiliation. Even their own families frequently blamed them for their joblessness. Why should this have been so? Does it suggest anything about the nature of American "individualism"?

From Mirra Komarovsky, The Unemployed Man and His Family: The Effect of Unemployment upon the Status of the Man in Fifty-nine Families *(New York: Dryden Press, 1940), 74-77.*

The Role of the Family Provider and the Self-Esteem of the Man. It is the man's duty to provide for the family. This pattern is apparently taken for granted by the cultural group to which our families belong. What does this role as a provider mean to the man? Does his self-esteem rest upon it? Does being the provider appear to him the core of his role in the family, the foundation upon which rests his claims to authority and respect? And, conversely, does loss of employment mean a profound sense of failure? Does it arouse fear for his status in the family?

The general impression that the interviews make is that in addition to sheer economic anxiety the man suffers from deep humiliation. He experiences a sense of deep frustration because in his own estimation he fails to fulfill what is the central duty of his life, the very touchstone of his manhood—the role of family provider. The man appears bewildered and humiliated. It is as if the ground had gone out from under his feet. He must have derived a profound sense of stability from having the family dependent upon him. Whether he had considerable authority within the family and was recognized as its head, or whether the wife's stronger personality had dominated the family, he nevertheless derived strength from his role as a provider. Every purchase of the family—the radio, his wife's new hat, the children's skates, the meals set before him—all were symbols of their dependence upon him. Unemployment changed it all. It is to the relief office, or to a relative, that the family now turns. It is to an uncle or a neighbor that the children now turn in expectation of a dime or a nickel for ice cream, or the larger beneficences such as a bicycle or an excursion to the amusement park.*

* Underlying the seriousness with which the man views his role as a provider is his general acceptance of the institution of the family and his responsibility for it. To the majority of the men the family was an unquestioned part of their lives. Not all of the men, of course, were competent providers prior to the depression. Some were shiftless and others drank heavily, but even these, however they may have rationalized their behavior in hot arguments with the wife or relatives, had a sense of guilt towards the family.

The feeling of disturbance and humiliation apparently exists irrespective of the intellectual convictions of the man. The men show different and almost contradictory verbal reactions to the situation. There are some who say, "If a child is well brought up, he will certainly not lose respect for his father just because his father happens to be out of work." Or, "Perhaps in foreign-born families children do lose respect for their unemployed fathers. It will not happen in any well-brought-up American family." Or, "A wife who would desert her husband just because he is unemployed is not worth a d——." Or, "I would break the children's necks if there was any hint of disrespect."

On the other hand, there were some who said, "It's only natural that the unemployed father should lose authority with the children." "Children's love must be bought." "Children love parents in gratitude for things that the parents do for them." "It's inevitable that the children will begin to wonder why their old man can't get a

Only a very few of the men wished they had never married. Mr. Jones said that if he had it all to do over again he would not marry. His idea of an ideal life was to knock around from one country to another, constantly seeking new fortunes and new adventures. Marriage tied him down. Mr. Kilpatrick said that he realized too late that he was not a family man. But he, incidentally, regrets his marriage, not because of the responsibilities it thrust upon him, but because he feels he was unfair to his wife and children and he considers it *his* defect that he cannot be faithful to one woman for a long time.

The majority, however, expressed no regrets concerning marriage, although in several cases they wished they had married different persons. Again and again both men and women wished they had not had so many children.

It doesn't mean, of course, that family life was a refuge and a blessing to the majority of the men. It may have been a burden, but if it was, it was so unquestioned and accepted a burden that the alternative of a single life did not exist in the consciousness. The answer to the question of what the man would do with one thousand dollars was quite revealing. Very few men said they would use the money to liberate themselves from the family. Those few said that they would first provide for the family and then go away and live independently—doing as they pleased and forgetting family troubles. But the majority of the men would spend the one thousand dollars within the family—establish a business, fix up the furniture, send the children to school, and so on.

job." "It is the father's job to provide for the family. The children can't help but resent it if he fails in his duty."

But whether the men said that it was natural or immoral and subversive for an unemployed man to lose status within the family, they felt equally disturbed by their plight.

The best way to describe the sense of uselessness and the anxiety of the men, their pathetic grasp at what little remains of their role as providers, is to let the men speak for themselves.

Profound, indeed, must be the importance of the role of the provider for the man's self-esteem to cause him to say, "I would rather starve than let my wife work." Or, "I would rather turn on the gas and put an end to the whole family than let my wife support me."

One man said that the worst thing about unemployment was having to go on relief. The next worst thing was having his wife work, as she had for a few months. To be supported by her, even for a short time, made him very unhappy. In fact, he is sure they would have drifted apart if she had continued longer. He would have left her. The whole thing was wrong. She was not the same; he was not the same. It was awful to have to ask her for tobacco, or to have to tell the landlady, "My wife will come, and I will pay you," or to be expected to have the dinner ready when she came home, or to have her too tired to talk to him at dinner. When he works and comes home tired, she is waiting for him and they have a nice talk together. But the other way it was quite different. At one time both of them worked. That was better. Then the one who got home first cooked the meal. But even that was all wrong.

It is interesting to see that in this particular family the wife is devoted to the husband and has attempted to make her employment as painless as possible for her husband. She tells this story:

When she first told her husband that she would look for work, he disapproved of it. She went right ahead. She could tell that every evening he was anxious until she told him that the search for work during the day had been fruitless. He could hardly conceal his pleasure. One day she did find a job in a department store. His first reaction was to tell her that in times of depression it is easier for a woman to find a job than it is for a man. She knew that he was unhappy and sulky, and tried to think of some way of reconciling him to her work. At the end of the first week she asked him to come to the store and meet some people she worked with, and also to help her carry the pay envelope home. He said he wouldn't come, but at closing time she found him waiting for her. After a while she noticed that he hated to have her pay the rent. She decided to let him pay the rent. Her sudden sickness made her discontinue working. She doesn't think he would have become reconciled to it had she continued for a long time.

One unemployed painter has a fine face which is lined with anxiety. He is 40 years old, but looks years older. He still has a position of authority in the family, but this doesn't allay his suffering. He feels that a father who is not a provider cannot possibly keep the love of the children. It was pathetic and significant to hear him repeat several times in the course of the interview that it was he who still provided the family with shelter and "kept the roof over their heads." "And isn't this, after all, the most important thing?" he appealed anxiously to the interviewer. He earned $25 a month as janitor of a church, and this money went for the rent of the family.

Not every man described his feelings so frankly and directly. There were many of the men who showed their anxieties only indirectly. One father, for example, forbade his children to play with other children of the neighborhood so that they would not make too many comparisons between him and the employed fathers of their friends. Another asked his wife at various intervals whether or not his children had said anything about his unemployment. One husband said that sex contacts with his wife were reduced on his initiative, while it is certain that it was his wife who insisted upon it.

Even the most intimate aspects of people's lives—their sexual relationships—were affected by the Depression. Did it affect men differently than women? Do the findings reported below suggest a connection between sex and general social and economic status? What did people in the 1930s appear to know about birth control? What was their attitude toward it?

From Mirra Komarovsky, The Unemployed Man and His Family: The Effect of Unemployment upon the Status of the Man in the Fifty-nine Families *(New York: Dryden Press, 1940), 130-33.*

The question arises as to how far the events of the depression changed the sex life of the couple. In many cases the interviewers found it difficult to approach the respondents on their sex life. Women were more able to question wives on this point, and men were more successful with husbands. Individuals differed very much in their ability to talk about their sex experiences.

The main question as to whether there has been any change at all during the depression in sex relations is answered affirmatively by most people. For 38 of the 59 cases information on sex was adequate. Of the 38, there were 16 that showed no change, while in 22 cases sex relations decreased in frequency, and in 4 of the 22 cases relations ceased altogether. No increases in frequency were noted, save in one case, in which the comment was made, "I think you want one another more when you're having hard luck than when everything is all right." It is safe then to say that sex life decreased, if it was affected at all.

In each case the respondent was asked for his or her reason for the change. Of the 22 families in which there was a decline, 8 claim that this came about for some reason not connected with the depression, such as ill health and the aging of the couple. But the remainder, 14, give some cause directly connected with the depression: fear of pregnancy was mentioned by 11 people, 2 said that relations were decreased because the wife lost respect for the husband because of the depression, and one claimed that "general anxiety" caused the decline.

It is evident that the alleged reasons may be merely convenient and socially acceptable excuses. It is hard to say what role the age of the couple played in the change. Comparison of the families in which there was no change in sex relations with those in which a decrease in frequency was observed shows that the latter are apt to be somewhat older.

Turning to unemployment as a possible cause of the decrease in frequency, we note that various aspects have operated to produce it: fear of pregnancy due to lack of money to provide for the mother and child, changes in the wife's attitude towards her husband, changes in the husband's attitude due to his economic frustration, or general anxiety and nervousness because of economic insecurity.

Fear of pregnancy seems to be a specter haunting many of these families. Eleven of them gave this as the reason for the decline in sex relations. These people apparently felt that merely by decreasing frequency of relations they avoided the danger of having children. Many of them felt that families on relief had no right to have more children. Their comments were such as these:

"It is a crime for children to be born when the parents haven't got enough money to have them properly."

"It is a crime for a man to bring children into the world in our circumstances."

"A man hasn't got a right to a child unless he can support him."

Ignorance of birth control added to the fear of pregnancy. Of the 31 for whom the information is available, 14 families use birth control, and 17 do not. Even among those who claim to practice some form of contraception there is a good deal of ignorance concerning the medically accepted practices. Only one family indicated that they had ever heard of a birth-control clinic, and only one woman had had medical advice on contraception. For the most part these people relied on over-the-back-fence methods. At least three families had had children while using these haphazard methods, and the feeling of the unreliability of any birth control device was prevalent. It is interesting, however, that five families increased their use of birth control during the depression. One man told his story thus:

"I could have avoided my present status if I had taken precautions to have fewer children. Before the depression I never gave a thought to birth control. Both my wife and I were against it, and let the children come as they would. Had we been able to foresee the depression, we would have felt differently about it. I'm convinced now that birth control is a good thing."

Among those who did not practice any form of contraception the confusion with regard to birth control was even greater. Some believed it caused cancer, confused it with some harmful practice, or thought it meant a State-enforced limitation of the family. Other couples opposed it only on religious grounds as "interference with nature."

Decline in sex relations may also be due to the loss of respect and affection for the unemployed husband. In some cases the failure of the husband affected the wife's response to him as a lover. This was apparently the situation in the Garland family:

Mrs. Garland said that her husband seemed a bigger man to her when he was employed and was making good money. Of course his unemployment had changed her attitude towards him. "When a man cannot provide for the family and makes you worry so, you lose your love for him. A husband has to have four qualifications—first, second, and third he should be able to support the family, and fourth he should have personality." Her husband doesn't fulfill any of these qualifications. If she had the money she would probably get a divorce. Mrs. Garland said she did enjoy sex relations prior to unemployment, but does not now. She herself does not understand the reason for the change. It is not because she is afraid of pregnancy. Perhaps it is because she lost her love for her husband.

Mrs. Garland is 30 years old and her husband is 34. There are some indications that Mrs. Garland is carrying on an affair with another man.

It will be remembered that in the Patterson family the husband complains that he does not get as much affection since loss of employment—that when he tells his wife he wants love she just gets mad. In the Dorrance family, marital relations at the present time are very strained. The family has been on relief for four years. The wife says that they have not had any sexual contacts for over three years. She can't bear the thought of his touching her. She is quite sure he has been unfaithful to her during this time, but she doesn't care.

Decline in the wife's response towards the husband is, however, not the only explanation. The wife who never enjoyed sex relations found in the husband's unemployment a convenient way out.

Fear of pregnancy was a convenient rationalization for Mrs. Fucini. She said that she had never enjoyed sex, and since unemployment she has managed to talk her husband into believing that it is too dangerous for the family to take the risk of having another child and besides they were too old for that sort of thing, anyway. (Mr. Fucini is 45 and Mrs. Fucini is 36.) He suggested that she go to a birth-control clinic, but she refused.

In only one case was there evidence that the initiative for the decrease in sex contacts came from the husband himself. In this family the husband was a quiet, introverted man of 40 years. He felt deeply his inability to provide for the family. He said, "It is awful to be old and discarded at 40. A man is not a man without work." At first his wife blamed him for unemployment, but later she realized that it was not his fault. In fact, she began to console him and plead with him not to torment himself with his failure as a provider. At the time of the interview the wife showed resentment against the husband, but this resentment was directed not against unemployment, but against his personal changes—the fact that he was gloomy, depressed, and didn't pay any attention to his wife. She gave the interviewer to understand that there were no sex contacts because the husband thought that they were too old. It is possible that his failure and his wife's reproaches had affected his sexual potency. At any rate it was at his initiative that sexual contacts were discontinued.

IV. WORK AND PLAY

Unemployment was not a new phenomenon in the 1930s. What was new was the scale of joblessness—the unprecedented numbers of men and women who could find no work. The following selections give some idea of the extent of the problem in 1934, the fifth year of the Depression. What steps was the government taking to deal with unemployment? How successful were they?

The table is from U.S. Bureau of the Census, Historical Statistics of the United States, Colonial Times to 1957 *(Washington: Government Printing Office, 1961), 73; the second selection is from* Fortune, *10 (October 1934), 55-56.*

The drama of unemployment that will be played this winter will be a stark and bitter drama, and one of the enigmas that you will notice as you watch it will be this: it will be very difficult to identify the villain. One group of spectators will insist that the villain is the machine, whose constantly improving technology operates constantly to throw new groups of unemployed upon the market. Another will argue that the villain was the War, which forced us to expand our capital plants beyond the necessities of normal peace-time consumption. Another will insist that if Mr. Roosevelt could only "reassure business" 5,000,000 men would be back at work within half a year. Another will insist that the villain is Capital which, by going on strike to maintain an impossible wage scale for itself, is depriving industry of the opportunity to produce goods. Some will dismiss all these to

UNEMPLOYMENT: 1900 to 1957

[In thousands of persons 14 years old and over. Annual averages]

Year	Unemployed (46)	Percent of civilian labor force (47)
1957	2,936	4.3
1956	2,551	3.8
1955	2,654	4.0
1954	3,230	5.0
1953	1,602	2.5
1952	1,673	2.7
1951	1,879	3.0
1950	3,142	5.0
1949	3,395	5.5
1948	2,064	3.4
1947	2,142	3.6
1946	2,270	3.9
1945	1,040	1.9
1944	670	1.2
1943	1,070	1.9
1942	2,660	4.7
1941	5,560	9.9
1940	8,120	14.6
1939	9,480	17.2
1938	10,390	19.0
1937	7,700	14.3
1936	9,030	16.9
1935	10,610	20.1
1934	11,340	21.7
1933	12,830	24.9
1932	12,060	23.6
1931	8,020	15.9
1930	4,340	8.7
1929	1,550	3.2
1928	2,080	4.4
1927	1,890	4.1
1926	880	1.9
1925	1,800	4.0
1924	2,440	5.5
1923	1,380	3.2
1922	3,220	7.6
1921	5,010	11.9
1920	1,670	4.0
1919	950	2.3
1918	560	1.4
1917	1,920	4.8
1916	1,920	4.8
1915	3,840	9.7
1914	3,110	8.0
1913	1,680	4.4
1912	1,960	5.2
1911	2,290	6.2
1910	2,150	5.9
1909	1,870	5.2
1908	2,960	8.5
1907	600	1.8
1906	280	0.8
1905	1,000	3.1
1904	1,490	4.8
1903	800	2.6
1902	800	2.7
1901	710	2.4
1900	1,420	5.0

claim that the villain is the U.S. tariff policy and the growth of economic insularity. And some will still blame it all on poor luckless Mr. Hoover—whose principal crime was that he was there when it happened.

TEN BASIC FACTS

Choose, then, your own villain; you have the fullest latitude. But anyone who wants to comprehend the magnitude of the stage on which the villain is stalking must set before himself ten basic facts and all but memorize them before he goes further. The ten basic facts of U.S. Unemployment in 1934 are these:

1. No one yet knows the true extent of unemployment, but the most widely accepted estimate placed the figure at 10,772,000 for July—down almost 3,000,000 from the all-time high, in March, 1933, of 13,689,000.

2. Since the average U.S. worker, for these statistical purposes, accounts for the support of two and one-half persons, the present unemployment figure means, roughly, that there are 27,000,000 people for whom private industry is no longer providing subsistence. Twenty-seven million people are 21 per cent of the country's population. (This figure would rise to 30 per cent if those inadequately supported—perhaps 10,000,000—were included.)

3. The actual relief load now being borne by federal, state, or local governments is 17,000,000. Donald Richberg asserts that the winter high will probably top 20,000,000. Subtract the present relief roll from the figure 27,000,000 above and learn that today there are still 10,000,000-odd who have no jobs over their heads but who have not *yet* been forced to apply for relief.

4. For this and similar reasons, relief rolls will probably rise constantly for another year at least, even should unemployment remain static or improve. And ahead stretch years in which the problem of reabsorbing any sizable fraction of this army on relief will grow steadily more complex.

5. The agency dealing out the great bulk of relief these days is the Federal Emergency Relief Administration. The Civilian Conservation Crops has taken some 350,000 families off the relief rolls but it

is not a fundamentally important agency, and with the demobilization of the Civil Works Administration last spring FERA assumed the brunt of the load.

6. Relief is provided in two forms—work relief and direct (cash or kind) relief. On work relief a man receives a wage (minimum thirty cents an hour) and works for three or more days, depending on the determination of his family's needs. But work relief is so much more expensive than direct relief—the dole, pure and simple—that only 5,000,000 individuals can benefit from it, as against more than 12,000,000 who must accept the dole.

7. The 17,000,000 on relief do not like the dole. They are almost unanimous in demanding *work*. They are bitter not only against the dole but against some of the sham work of work relief. Many a social disorder will center around the demand for work this winter.

8. Within FERA a new phenomenon has arisen—the Federal Surplus Relief Corporation. Beginning only as an agency to make possible the useful consumption of surplus farm products, it has now become an important part of the country's whole distributive mechanism—to supply the unemployed, over and above the cash relief they receive, with canned meat, blankets, mattresses, shoes, etc. Its present expenditures are between $6,000,000 and $11,000,000 a month.

9. About three-quarters of all relief expenditures are now borne by the federal government; total public expenditures for relief are now running about $130,000,000 a month. States in general are weak contributors; communities do better than their states, and although private charity still works manfully, it is no longer able to contribute even 5 per cent of the total relief funds needed.

10. It is questionable whether unaided private industry in the last year has been responsible for *any* net reëmployment. Most of the industrial reëmployment (1,000,000-odd workers) that took place between July, 1933, and July, 1934, is attributable to indirect work created by PWA projects. Between these two dates industry's burden rose—and fell. Against the much publicized expansion in certain businesses last year, many others have been quietly laying off men this summer.

We think of unemployment as an urban, industrial phenomenon, but it had its impact on farmers as well, as prices fell and crops could find no markets. What was the aspect of the situation that most puzzled Oscar Ameringer, whose testimony to a Congressional Committee in 1932 is printed below? If there were as much discontent as he claims to have found, why do you think there was no "revolution" in the 1930s?

From Unemployment in the United States: Hearings before a Subcommittee of the Committee on Labor, *House of Representatives, Seventy-Second Congress, First Session (Washington: Government Printing Office, 1932), 97-101.*

STATEMENT OF OSCAR AMERINGER, EDITOR OF THE
AMERICAN GUARDIAN, OKLAHOMA CITY, OKLA.

Mr. JACOBSEN. You may proceed.

Mr. AMERINGER. My name is Oscar Ameringer. I am editor of the American Guardian and former editor of the American Miner. I live in Oklahoma City, Okla.

I may say that I am a representative of the country at large. During the last four months I have visited more than 20 States in my capacity as a newspaper man and an observer of prevailing conditions. Now, the witnesses that have preceded me have told you about a deplorable condition among the unemployed. They have told you of exhausted city treasuries and exhausted charity funds. They have told you about rising needs and falling incomes. They have told you about mothers being emaciated and not being able to give milk to their offspring. They have told you about infants being fed for months on flour and water. You have heard the young miner from Pennsylvania tell about conditions in his section of the country. You have heard the young miner from the State of West Virginia tell of conditions in his country. Both of these men have served their country trying to make the country safe for democracy.

The governments of their respective States, West Virginia and Pennsylvania, have done all in their power to bring in unions of these men, their only protections, and reduce their wages to a starvation level and incidentally make beggars out of World War heroes.

I know these men have told you the truth. And in my former capacity of editor of the American Miner I have received thousands of letters telling of similar and even worse conditions. What they have told you, however, is that their plight could be multiplied by hundreds of thousands.

In the year 1921 the Miners' Union of Illinois was composed of 90,000 men. At the end of 1930 this membership had fallen to 50,000. Of these, 25,000 men were exonerated from the payment of dues on account of unemployment. In this connection it must be remembered that so long as a man works two days for pay—that is 2 days out of 15—he is regarded as employed.

During the last decade some 20,000 families were driven from the coal regions in Illinois alone. Credit and savings had been used long before the stock market crash of 1929. Those who had homes or equities in homes have lost them. What the years of shrinking employment have not devoured bank failures have, taking with them not only the meager savings of the most frugal and lucky but also the funds of these unions.

To-day there are counties in the once so prosperous mining fields of Illinois that do not contain one single bank, as Mr. Keller here will corroborate. In the county Mr. Keller comes from it is my recollection that there is not a single bank left there. In fact, I do not believe there are any banks left in that coal-mining region. I was in Christian County, and, as I remember, there is not a single one left.

If I had the time I would enumerate some of the causes leading to this disaster involving perhaps 3,000,000 human beings, if we include the coal fields of the Mississippi Valley alone.

Needless to say, the plight of these people is totally undeserved. They are victims of circumstances over which they had no control. Nor can their sufferings be attributed to the so-called acts of God, for while they and many other millions of brother toilers were suffering from the lack of decent necessities of life, food and raw material for clothing were rotting or were destroyed by the millions of tons.

During the last three months I have visited, as I have said, some 20 States of this wonderfully rich and beautiful country. Here are some of the things I heard and saw: In the State of Washington I was told that the forest fires raging in that region all summer and fall were caused by unemployed timber workers and bankrupt farmers in an endeavor to earn a few honest dollars as fire fighters. The last thing I saw on the night I left Seattle was numbers of women searching for scraps of food in the refuse piles of the principal market of that city. A number of Montana citizens told me of thousands of bushels of wheat left in the fields uncut on account of its low price that hardly paid for the harvesting. In Oregon I saw thousands of bushels of apples rotting in the orchards. Only absolute flawless apples were still salable, at from 40 to 50 cents a box containing 200 apples. At the same time, there are millions of children who, on account of the poverty of their parents, will not eat one apple this winter.

While I was in Oregon the Portland Oregonian bemoaned the fact that thousands of ewes were killed by the sheep raisers because they did not bring enough in the market to pay the freight on them. And while Oregon sheep raisers fed mutton to the buzzards, I saw men picking for meat scraps in the garbage cans in the cities of New York and Chicago. I talked to one man in a restaurant in Chicago. He told me of his experience in raising sheep. He said that he had killed 3,000 sheep this fall and thrown them down the canyon, because it cost $1.10 to ship a sheep, and then he would get less than a dollar for it. He said he could not afford to feed the sheep, and he would not let them starve, so he just cut their throats and threw them down the canyon.

The roads of the West and Southwest teem with hungry hitchhikers. The camp fires of the homeless are seen along every railroad track. I saw men, women, and children walking over the hard roads. Most of them were tenant farmers who had lost their all in the late slump in wheat and cotton. Between Clarksville and Russellville, Ark., I picked up a family. The woman was hugging a dead chicken under a ragged coat. When I asked her where she had procured the fowl, first she told me she had found it dead in the road, and then added in grim humor, "They promised me a chicken in the pot, and now I got mine."

In Oklahoma, Texas, Arkansas, and Louisiana I saw untold bales of cotton rotting in the fields because the cotton pickers could not keep body and soul together on 35 cents paid for picking 100 pounds. The farmers cooperatives who loaned the money to the planters to make the crops allowed the planters $5 a bale. That means 1,500 pounds of seed cotton for the picking of it, which was in the neighborhood of 35 cents a pound. A good picker can pick about 200 pounds of cotton a day, so that the 70 cents would not provide enough pork and beans to keep the picker in the field, so that there is fine staple cotton rotting down there by the hundreds and thousands of tons.

As a result of this appalling overproduction on the one side and the staggering underconsumption on the other side, 70 per cent of the farmers of Oklahoma were unable to pay the interests on their mortgages. Last week one of the largest and oldest mortgage companies in that State went into the hands of the receiver. In that and other States we have now the interesting spectacle of farmers losing their farms by foreclosure and mortgage companies losing their recouped holdings by tax sales.

The farmers are being pauperized by the poverty of industrial populations and the industrial populations are being pauperized by the poverty of the farmers. Neither has the money to buy the product of the other, hence we have overproduction and underconsumption at the same time and in the same country.

I have not come here to stir you in a recital of the necessity for relief for our suffering fellow citizens. However, unless something is done for them and done soon, you will have a revolution on hand. And when that revolution comes it will not come from Moscow, it will not be made by the poor communists whom our police are heading up regularly and efficiently. When the revolution comes it will bear the label "Laid in the U. S. A." and its chief promoters will be the people of American stock.

Had I known a few days sooner that I would appear before your committee I should have secured a number of letters that have reached me during the last six months in my capacity as editor of the American Guardian. However, my fellow Oklahoman, Mr. J. A. Simpson, president of the Farmers' Union, was kind enough last night to loan me a few of the 16,000 that have reached him in answer to a radio address he made a few weeks ago.

Mr. AMERINGER. I will not give the names of the writers of these letters. The first one says:

The way I feel now, with a few exceptions such as Frazier, Wheeler, Norris, Shipstead, McFadden, and such, the rest of them could be lined up against an adobe wall in front of a machine-gun corps and that corps would be the most patriotic group this country has ever produced, if good shots.

The next letter says, in part:

I can not help but think of conditions in France that led up to the revolution, and I begin to wonder and fear we are rushing to the same or similar end. The people will be robbed and trodden under foot just so long. Then woe to those oppressors who have brought a people to the limit of endurance and roused their wrathful vengeance; and it matters little whether the mighty have built their power on royal sod or shining gold.

The next letter says, in part:

* * * as many of our farmers to-day are on the verge of resorting to things you and I would not be guilty of * * *

Next:

The U. S. A. absolutely very soon will come to a moral and honest basis or there is going to be hell. I have heard many state that they didn't have the least desire to go to Europe to fight, but were now ready to fight. One hates to hear them words, but the true spirit of our people is swaying. Greed means destruction.

The next letter says:

Just a word picture. I am 48; married 21 years; four children, three in school. I have never been arrested or even in the newspapers. For the last eight years I was employed as a Pullman conductor. Since September, 1930, they have given me seven months part-time work. To-day I am an object of charity. Till now I have never subscribed to radical actions of Bolshevik thoughts, and this is the first letter of this nature I have ever written, but my small, weak, and frail wife and two small children are suffering and I have come to that terrible place where I could easily resort to violence in my desperation.

The next letter says:

People the country over are thinking along serious lines these days. If it were not for their belief in God and His promises, "Vengeance is mine, I will repay, saith the Lord," I wonder sometimes just what would happen. If the politicians and capitalists do not awaken to the true feelings of the masses, those downtrodden may forget all and take vengeance in their own hands. Sometimes it seems all they need would be a great fearless leader like Joshua or Moses.

The next letter says:

I hope your talk will open the eyes of the people of the United States and those who represent them at Washington who have a guilty conscience to aid foreign nations instead of giving assistance to our own Nation may not return to our Nation's Capitol again.

Next:

Out of the black mire up to the highest mountain tops with our Star-Spangled Banner that we have fought and died for.

Lastly, one man writes:

Now, I don't care whether I develop oil or fight; if it is fight, let's get together and do the job right and never let up.

Let me say, as you know, that our State is very rich in oil, as is Texas, and for some months past with us oil has been selling for less than water. Where they have not got drinking water they have to haul it in barrels, and lately a barrel of water has been worth 25 cents, whereas a barrel of oil has been worth only 15 cents.

Some time ago a cowman came into my office in Oklahoma City.

He was one of these double-fisted gentlemen, with the gallon hat and all. He said, "You do not know me from Adam's ox." I said, "No; I do not believe I know you." He said, "But I know you and I used to hear you make speeches, and I came to tell you that I used to think you were a darned fool, but now I know I am the fool." I asked, "What has happened?" He said, "I came to this country without a cent, but, knowing my onions, and by tending strictly to business, I finally accumulated two sections of land and a fine herd of white-faced Hereford cattle. I was independent." I remarked that anybody could do that if he worked hard and did not gamble and used good management. He said, "After the war cattle began to drop, and I was feeding them corn, and by the time I got them to Chicago the price of cattle, considering the price of corn I had fed them, was not enough to even pay my expenses. I could not pay anything."

Continuing, he said, "I mortgaged my two sections of land, and to-day I am cleaned out; by God, I am not going to stand for it." I asked him what he was going to do about it, and he said, "We have got to have a revolution here like they had in Russia and clean them up." I finally asked him, "Who is going to make the revolution?" He said, "I just want to tell you that I am going to be one of them, and I am going to do my share in it." I asked what his share was and he said, "I will capture a certain fort. I know I can get in with 20 of my boys," meaning his cowboys, "because I know the inside and outside of it, and I capture that with my men." I rejoined, "Then what?" He said, "We will have 400 machine guns, so many batteries of artillery, tractors, and munitions and rifles, and everything else needed to supply a pretty good army." Then I asked, "What then?" He said, "If there are enough fellows with guts in this country to do like us, we will march eastward and we will cut the East off. We will cut the East off from the West. We have got the granaries; we have the hogs, the cattle, the corn, and East has nothing but mortgages on our places. We will show them what we can do."

That man may be very foolish, and I think he is, but he is in dead earnest, he is a hard-shelled Baptist and a hard-shelled Democrat, not a Socialist or a Communist, but just a plain American cattleman whose ancestors went from Carolina to Tennessee, then to Arkansas, and then to Oklahoma. I have heard much of this talk from serious-minded prosperous men of other days.

As you know, talk is always a mental preparation for action. Nothing is done until people talk and talk and talk it, and they finally get the notion that they will do it.

I do not say we are going to have a revolution on hand within the next year or two, perhaps never. I hope we may not have such; but the danger is here. That is the feeling of our people—as reflected in the letters I have read. I have met these people virtually every day all over the country. There is a feeling among the masses generally that something is radically wrong. They are despairing of political action. They say the only thing you do in Washington is to take money from the pockets of the poor and put it into the pockets of the rich. They say that this Government is a conspiracy against the common people to enrich the already rich. I hear such remarks every day.

Oscar Ameringer apparently did not travel to the deep South in 1932. In the following selection, however, Congressman George Huddleston describes the situation in Alabama in that year. What were the special features of Southern life that aggravated the effects of the Depression on many people there?

From Unemployment Relief: Hearings before a Subcommittee of the Committee on Manufactures, *United States Senate, Seventy-Second Congress, First Session (Washington: Government Printing Office, 1932), 244-45.*

There is another aspect of this thing that I want to mention. I come from a part of the country that is poor, not from any lack of quality on the part of our people, but due to causes going back a good many years that I will not attempt to discuss. The accumulations of wealth throughout the Southeastern States are quite small, much smaller than in any other section of the country, and quite ridiculous compared to that of some rich communities in the United States.

We have a great many tenant farmers there. We have a great many negro farmers, and practically all of them are tenants. Their ability to survive, to eat, to have a shelter, depends upon the ability of the landlord to supply them with the necessaries of life. They have a system under which they make a contract with the landlord to cultivate his land for the next year and in the meantime he feeds them through the winter, and at the end of the year they gather their crops and pay for their supplies and rent, if they are able to do so. Conditions in agriculture have been such for several years that the landlords have been gradually impoverished and their farms are mortgaged to the farm-loan system and to the mortgage companies in a multitude of instances.

In a very large percentage the landlord is now unable to finance these tenants for another year. He is unable to get the supplies. He has no security and no money with which to feed and clothe his tenants until they can make another crop. They came to the end of the season—their chief crop is cotton which they sold at from 5 to 6 cents, and very few of them were able to pay for the supplies that it required for them to make the crop. They owe the landlord. Many landlords have said to them, generously, "Keep what you have made and go your way. I can not feed you another year. You will have to do the best you can, but keep whatever you have made." A great many of these landlords, no matter how well intentioned, are incapable of financing these tenants another year. The landlord is in almost as bad shape as the tenant. He owed for the supplies. He had to take what he received at the end of the season and turn it over to the merchant, or to the bank to pay them what he owed. He has been unable to pay in full, so that he can not advance them another year. Many of these people, especially the negro tenants, are now in the middle of a winter, practically without food and without clothes, and without anything else, and how are they going to live? Many of these local counties have no charitable organizations. They are poor people and impoverished. They have no county funds. There is no place to turn, nobody that has any money that they can turn to and ask for help.

Many white people are in the same kind of a situation. They beg around among their neighbors. The neighbors are poor and they have no means of helping them. They stray here and there.

Any thought that there has been no starvation, that no man has starved, and no man will starve, is the rankest nonsense. Men are actually starving by the thousands to-day, not merely in the general sections that I refer to, but throughout this country as a whole, and in my own district. I do not mean to say that they are sitting down and not getting a bite of food until they actually die, but they are living such a scrambling, precarious existence, with suffering from lack of clothing, fuel, and nourishment, until they are subject to be swept away at any time, and many are now being swept away.

The situation has possibilities of epidemics of various kinds. Its consequences will be felt many years. The children are being stunted by lack of food. Old people are having their lives cut short. The physical effects of the privations that they are forced to endure will not pass away within 50 years and when the social and civic effects will pass away, only God knows. That is something that no man can estimate.

Even for those who still had jobs, income was often reduced. While wages and salaries fell, prices did not, or fell more slowly and not so far. The author of the following selection was evidently a moderately prosperous, probably white-collar, worker before the Depression. While pinched, he did not suffer so badly as many. In what ways did the Depression alter his standard of living? Which items does he consider necessities, and which luxuries? From his budget, how can we reconstruct a picture of a "middle-class" way of life in the 1930s?

From James R. Martin, " 'Buy Now'—on $30 a week," The Nation, *137 (November 1, 1933),* 502-03.

"BUY NOW"—ON $30 A WEEK

by James R. Martin

Our local NRA [National Recovery Administration] committee has just started a "Buy Now" campaign. We are urged to increase our buying to the limit, so that factories can be busy again and the millions of unemployed be put back at work. I wish I could buy more, but I can't. My total earnings of $2,500 a year in 1929 have shrunk to about $1,500 today. But many of my expenses have not shrunk at all. That is the reason I cannot buy more, and am, indeed, on the road to ruin. If my case were an exception, it would be just my hard luck. However, I think it is typical of the situation in which the great mass of consumers find themselves today. I suspect my own decline in income of 40 per cent since 1929 represents just about the national average.

Prices have not come down with incomes. Food, clothing, merchandise have fallen substantially, yes. But I still pay 1929 boom-time prices for mortgage interest, taxes, telephone, electricity and gas, bus and commuting fares, movies, insurance, doctors and dentists, and coal, and fairly high prices for gasoline and motor oil, tobacco and cigarettes, and ice.

In 1926 I bought an $8,000 house and borrowed a $4,000 mortgage. I am still paying 6 per cent on that $4,000, despite the fact that the mortgagee lent me dollars that were inflated and wouldn't buy so much, while I have to pay him now in dollars that can buy a great deal more. Of my $30 weekly earnings, I have to pay almost $5 for this interest.

My tax bill did not fall at all during the first three years of the depression, and this year was reduced only 10 per cent. Taxes take almost $3.60 each week.

Telephone rates are the same as they were in 1929. The stockholders are still receiving the high dividend of 9 per cent on their money, the bond-holders are still getting the same interest, and the officials and employees, after "suffering" a temporary salary reduction of 10 per cent in the past year, have just had their pay restored to its boom-time levels. None of these classes know that there is a depression, but the customers do.

Electric and gas rates are still the same, although the company advertises that it has made reductions. My bill on a weekly basis runs to about $1.25. The company's bond-holders are receiving their interest in full, the common-stock dividends were paid right up to a few months ago, and the salaries of officials and employees have been reduced only 15 per cent.

Bus fares remain high. Before the war the street-car company charged five cents flat over a sizable region. Now the bus company charges ten, fifteen, or twenty cents, according to zones, and declares that it is losing money. The company attempted to obtain a State-wide monopoly and bought out one independent bus system after another at fancy prices. In this way it ran up a huge bonded debt, and now claims that the heavy interest charge on this debt makes lower bus fares impossible. Yet it makes no attempt to lower these charges, takes good care of the stockholders, and pays high salaries to a large number of officials.

Motion pictures are a necessity rather than a luxury. The three theaters in our town charged forty cents in boom times and made money. Two of them were leased at a high rent and for a long term by a large motion-picture producing company, which immediately raised the price to fifty cents and has kept it there. I suppose that besides the high rents it also must pay heavy bond-interest charges, a host of high-salaried officials, and dividends on at least the preferred stock. If these movie admissions had fallen as much as my income has since 1929, they would be twenty-five cents today. The third theater is a neighborhood institution that still charges forty cents as it did in 1929. The manager told me the price of admission could not be reduced because the producers still charge 1929 prices for films, and the theater building is under a long-term lease fixed in the high-price years. The theater company is owned by three New Yorkers who spend their winter vacations in Florida.

The railroad which carries many local commuters to New York every day has not only refused to lower rates but raised them 15 per cent. The railroad asserts that it carries the commuters at a loss. The fact is that for ten years the civic interests of the State have been trying, after extensive studies by experts, to persuade the railroads in this area to pool their commuting business in a unified, electrified rapid-transit system. This would mean profit instead of loss to the railroads, and a saving of time for the commuters. The railroads, jealous of their individual independence, have refused to do this, and the passengers pay the cost in time and money.

Coal is still around $14 a ton in this area. The coal bill is an important one in the consumer's budget; for me it amounts to about $2.10 a week. Oil for my automobile is about what it was in 1929.

Gasoline is back to eighteen cents a gallon, which is only two cents away from the five gallons for a dollar of boom days. Both cost me about $2 a week. So many petroleum companies have sunk wells that cutthroat competition has resulted, and five months ago the price of gas went down to eleven cents. Then the companies all got together under the NRA code, restricted production, fixed a "fair price," and gas shot up to eighteen cents a gallon.

Cigarettes at twelve cents a package have fallen 20 per cent since 1929, or only half of the fall in my income. Probably that is the reason why some of these tobacco companies have until recently been able to pay million-dollar bonuses to certain executives, and why the National City Bank in a recent survey stated that the tobacco manufacturers had been able to maintain their boom-time profits more successfully than any other line of business.

I had a tooth pulled recently. The dentist charged me $4 for two X-ray views and $5 for pulling the tooth. These were the same rates he charged four years ago. Doctors' and dentists' bills for us average $1.25 a week. The rates are still high.

A decent lunch costs almost as much as it did in 1929. The reductions have been astonishingly small. In drugstores ice-cream sodas and sundaes and coffee still cost the old high prices. Many of these places complain of the high rent they still have to pay on account of long-term leases contracted when rentals were fabulous. The more fundamental reason, it seems to me, is that there are far too many eating places and drugstores. Each gets so small a share of the available business that it has to charge high prices to make ends meet. One would think that competition between all these places would lower prices until it drove the excess number out of business. It doesn't work out that way. These businesses have learned to keep prices at a certain level. It is another case of the consumer having to support too many firms.

All these things cost us $20 a week. They cost us the same amount in 1929. There has been no reduction. But then I was earning $50 a week and these necessities were only 40 per cent of my income. Now I am making only $30 a week and they are 66 per cent of my income. I had $30 left over then. I have only $10 left now. After paying a reduced amount for food and cheap shoes, I have nothing with which to buy the clothing, furniture, rugs, automobiles, books, lamps, and other merchandise whose production would keep our factories busy and restore employment to millions. That is why the factories are largely idle. The consumers have nothing left with which to buy merchandise after they have paid tribute to mortgage and bond owners, electric-light and gas companies, bus and railroad systems, coal barons, motion-picture producers, doctors and dentists, and the oil and gas price-fixing combine.

What can I buy? A new automobile or even a second-hand one is out of the question for me. I shall have to continue using my five-year-old car. I know clothing prices have declined, but I am wearing a slightly worn suit which I bought from my brother for $10. My last pair of shoes was purchased eight months ago. I have not bought a necktie for two years. The radio has worn out and we haven't reached the point where we can spare $15 for a new one. We haven't bought any furniture or house furnishings for four years. We do not patronize plays, concerts, or big games. Summer vacations are no longer possible, and a weekend trip would cost money we couldn't afford. We have even cut down on food—less meat, cake, ice cream, soft drinks, candy.

Our expenses are more than our income. That is why our savings have gone down to a few hundred dollars in the bank against illness or disaster. The securities we had were sold two years ago at a loss. We have begun to borrow on our insurance. The taxes for 1933 are not yet paid and probably won't be. We can discontinue the telephone, but the automobile is a business necessity. If you think we haven't been thrifty, try and run a home on $30 a week.

Now we find that prices are going up again, although our income is not. The NRA is supposed to increase employment and raise wages. Several million of the unemployed are back at work, it is true, but the wage level has not risen, except in a few industries. The minimum wage has too often been made a maximum wage as well. The point I wish to make is that a rise in wages and incomes may still be a long way off. Meanwhile, the burden of having to pay 1929 prices for so many necessities is crushing us—and making it impossible for us to "Buy Now."

The following selection consists of several short case histories of families on relief. What did unemployment mean in the lives of these families? Did it affect their place of residence? Their possessions? Their savings? What kinds of alternative income could these families find? How did they try to cut costs? What was their attitude toward the welfare system?

From Federal Aid for Unemployment Relief, Hearings before a Subcommittee of the Committee on Manufactures on S. 5125, *United States Senate, Seventy-second Congress, Second Session (Washington: Government Printing Office, 1933), 507-09.*

STATEMENT BY EDWARD D. LYNDE, GENERAL SECRETARY OF THE ASSOCIATED CHARITIES, CLEVELAND, OHIO

I wish to insert in the record at this time a group of brief summaries of case histories of family situations known to the Associated Charities, of Cleveland, received to-day from Edward D. Lynde, general secretary of the Cleveland Associated Charities, to illustrate the distress caused in individual families by widespread and prolonged unemployment. The names and other identifying data concerning these families have, of course, been changed or withheld.

(The papers referred to are printed in full as follows:)

FAMILY PROBLEMS AND UNEMPLOYMENT

Davis: Karl, 44; Mary, 40; Evelyn, 21; and Elsie, 20.

The family has been known to Associated Charities because of unemployment since February 26, 1932. Mr. Davis earned $30 a week until about a year before applying for aid. The family exhausted all of their resources before coming to Associated Charities and have made every effort to cooperate with the agency. They once had a nice home, a piano, radio, and nice furniture. They are now living in four small rooms in a colored section of the city. All members of the family feel this change in standards keenly.

Evelyn has been ill a great deal. She had chorea when a child and is still quite frail. She had most of her upper teeth removed several months ago and has not been able to have them replaced and is quite self-conscious about her appearance.

Relief is being given to supplement the income of Elsie, who earns $5 a week doing housework. The family borrowed from practically all of their relatives before applying to Associated Charities and are entirely without resources other than Elsie now.

Walters: Joseph, 33; Ida, 24; Frederick, 5; and Joseph, 3.

This family applied for relief after Mr. Walters had been laid off his job, which he had held for four years. The family has a very high standard of living and are deeply religious. Formerly they had a very nice home but recently they had had to move into the home of a relative.

Prior to being laid off in 1930, Mr. Walters earned $20 to $25 a week, and his wife earned $11 per week. At present there is no income, but once in a great while Mr. Walters' former employer will give him a half day's work for some specific article that is needed in the home.

The family owes approximately $35 at the present time for lights, gas, and rent. The weekly food order amounts to $2.70, and by careful planning the family has been able to get along on this. There are gifts of vegetables from friends occasionally to help out. We have also assisted recently with underthings and children's clothing.

D'Amico: Enrico, 45; Philomena, 43; and Antoinette, 15.

The D'Amico family only recently applied for Associated Charities assistance although Mr. D'Amico has been out of work for over a year and a half. They lived on their savings during this time, proud of the fact that they did not have to apply for charity. The depression has lasted too long for their meager savings. This family has always maintained a high standard of living. It is reflected in the children and in the home. The older girls attend John Hay High School. They are a little ahead of their class and do very good work. Antoinette, who is a very intelligent girl, has been troubled for the past year and a half with severe headaches and this is attributed to her eye condition, as she needs glasses very badly.

Kish: Andrew, 46; Anna, 44; Daniel, 19; Olga, 17; Eddie, 15; and Matilda, 13.

Mr. Kish has been employed by the Hupp Motor Car Corporation for a number of years as a duco finisher but was laid off three years ago because of unemployment, and has not been able to secure work since. He is hard of hearing and this serves as a handicap to further employment. For a while the family got along very nicely since they have been quite provident and had purchased a home. In the fall of 1932 the bank foreclosed. When all of the family resources were exhausted, they made application to the Associated Charities. Unemployment relief has been given since the first of December.

Olga is attending West High School. She is an unusually attractive girl and is both active and interested in school affairs. Although her clothing is very poor, she has maintained her school activities in a very wholesome fashion. Unless some special opportunity is provided for her on a scholarship basis, she will have to stop school at the end of this term as the family can not afford to buy her books, car fare, and lunches.

Tekesky: Joseph, 30; Mary, 28; Lillian, 5; Junior, 2-1/2; and Evelyn, 1.

The above-named family has been known to the Associated Charities since December 15, 1930. Mr. Tekesky is a carpenter but has been unemployed since that date. He has tried to secure any kind of a job but has been unsuccessful.

Mrs. Tekesky has become quite discouraged because of Mr. Tekesky's unemployment. She has high standards of housekeeping but the house is meagerly furnished and is badly in need of bedding.

There is no income in the home as Mr. Tekesky has not been able to secure any odd jobs. Previous to this period of unemployment Mr. Tekesky earned an adequate income, approximately $60 per week. There are no friends or relatives who can be of any possible assistance. Mr. Tekesky's parents have assisted the family but they can do no more. The family is greatly in debt for grocery, gas, and light bills.

Mathew: John, 44; Julius, 16; and Vincent, 12.

Mr. Matthew has been unemployed since last spring when he was let out of a city job. Since that time he has tried to keep the home together and be both father and mother to the boys. He cooks for them and even does the washing, and is quite proud of the way he irons their clothes. Mr. Matthew is very anxious that the boys get as good an education as is possible, and Julius, age 16, enjoys going to school very much and is very much interested in his business course at West Tech. He is in the third year and has been having a very difficult time this year getting the necessary supplies for his bookkeeping course. Occasionally he has been able to earn 50 cents on Saturday peddling hand bills, but he does not have this success very often. He has borrowed books and school supplies from the other boys, but does not feel that he could possibly go through another year doing this.

Mr. Matthew's sister helps the family as much as possible and manages to keep the boys fairly comfortably dressed for school, but can not always contribute for Julius' school materials, as they are rather expensive for the type of course that he is taking. He is a very studious boy and is greatly worried because he may have to stop school in February because his father has no money to buy the necessary books and supplies for him.

Associated Charities is furnishing a weekly grocery order of $2.15 and flour. Coal is also sent, and kerosene is provided monthly.

In order for Julius to continue at West Tech it is quite necessary that he have some means of securing the necessary supplies, as the school has no way of taking care of this. He does not object about having to walk to school or carry his lunch.

Priesly: Richard, 24; Mary, 22; and Dolores, 21 months.

This small family has been through a hectic two years since their wedding day. Both parental families are unable to assist them financially. Although they have been known to the Associated Charities for over a year, Mr. Priesly has been partially self-supporting during that time. The fact that they were forced to stay with his parents, a large family in crowded quarters, gave them little privacy and less security. As soon as Mr. Priesly secured his last job, they moved into furnished rooms.

They were hoping to move later into unfurnished rooms but Mr. Priesly's health was affected by the lead fumes in the shop where he worked and he was obliged to give up this job before these plans could be carried out. The Associated Charities helped to establish them, however, and Mrs. Priesly is happy at last to have their own home. Her parents keep a much better home than Mr. Priesly's parents. Thus it was difficult for her to adjust herself to the squalor and the noise of that temporary refuge. She managed to do it, though, without any friction. The family are now living in three small rooms downstairs in an old 4-family house and the Associated Charities is giving full relief. Both Mr. and Mrs. Priesly are anxious to be as independent of charity as possible.

There is no income in the family at present, however, nor are they able to secure help from their families. At the same time, they are relatively free from debt, owing only the bill for Mrs. Priesly's confinement during the birth of Dolores.

The Associated Charities is giving a weekly grocery order of $3.50, clothes when needed, and 25 per cent of the rent regularly. Some few items were also provided for the home. Mrs. Priesly's mother donated the greater portion of the few bits of furniture.

The kitchen has been adapted to serve as the main room. Dolores is at the age when she spends most of her playing time on the floor. The numerous cracks and crannies in it expose her to cold and dampness, at the same time making the room hard to heat. We are asking for $3.50 to buy a linoleum rug for the kitchen.

Petocky: John, 45; Sophia, 44; Edmond, 15; Raymond, 13; Teddy, 8; Eugene, 5; Irene, 2-1/2; and Matthew, 6 months.

The Petocky's home is a tiny 5-room cottage set in the middle of a large garden. During the course of many years that the family has lived there they have repaired and rebuilt the house so that from a shanty it has become a home. To them it represents all that they had hoped to gain in coming to America. Now, they fear to lose this property because for many months no payments have been made on the mortgage.

Associated Charities supplies all families' necessities—food, clothing, and fuel. Twice Associated Charities has paid interest on the mortgage: $9.60 on July 30, 1931, and $9.99 on January 25, 1932, to prevent foreclosure. The bank is again threatening.

When employed in the contracting business before the depression,

Mr. Petocky earned $7 a day. Since April, 1930, he has had no work; consequently family has no income at all. There are no relatives to assist.

Archer: Charles, 33; Hilda, 23; Charles, 1; and Mrs. Archer's father, Mr. Rowe.

Neither Mr. Archer nor Mr. Rowe have had work for many months. Mr. Rowe is especially anxious to get work and would do anything. He was for many years a chauffeur in Germany and is very proud of the fact that he knows so much about cars. He is very unhappy because he is forced to live with his daughter when he ought to be able to care for himself.

Duncan: Frank, 44; Agnes, 40; Frank, 23; Alvina, 21; Milan, 18; Daisy, 14; Esther, 10; and Iona May, 8.

The Duncan family came to the attention of the Associated Charities because of Mr. Duncan's unemployment. He was laid off from work because of illness. He then went back to work again until a few months ago, when he was laid off because of lack of work.

The home life of the family is of a high order and they are devoted to one another. The family have been accustomed to a higher standard of living and therefore, it has been difficult for them to meet a lower standard but both Mr. and Mrs. Duncan are cooperative in this regard. Mrs. Duncan tries to be cheerful in order to keep up the family's morale. She complains of ill health but she is nervous and becomes excited very easily.

Before Mr. Duncan was laid off entirely he was earning on an average of $16 every two weeks. Alvina worked at the Ohio Bell Telephone Co. but has been unemployed for the past year. There is no income in the home at present. Neither Mr. nor Mrs. Duncan have any relatives who can assist the family.

Associated Charities has been assisting the family with a $5 weekly grocery order and has also given one sack of flour each week.

One week ago a furniture company took away some of the family's furniture, including a mattress. Since then it has been necessary for the children to sleep on the floor.

Perhaps curiously, the 1930s, which saw so many people out of work, also witnessed a widespread concern for the quality of work and working conditions. In the following selection, one worker describes an average day on the assembly line, a form of employment that was increasingly typical of a large-scale industrial society. Could workers like Gene Richard (who also identifies himself by his time-clock number) derive any personal satisfaction from their jobs? What do you think the psychological effects of such employment must have been? Did it exploit human beings? What benefits did it provide?

From Gene Richard (Time-Clock No. 1135284), "On the Assembly Line," The Atlantic Monthly, 159 (April, 1937), 424-28.

[GENE RICHARD—it is his real name—is an automobile worker twenty-three years old, weighing one hundred and thirty-five pounds and standing five foot seven. He describes the effect of mechanical pacing, in the assembly line, upon his mind and nerves. He is probably more sensitive to the strain of routine operations than the average automobile worker; before entering the factory he had some slight experience as a professional musician. Again, he is not typical because he is more articulate in expression than most of his mates, few of whom could identify and express the tensions which harass them. The fatigues which he describes are not those of muscles, but of nerves. They arise, perhaps, from the fact that man as a physical organism is made for sudden bursts of swift energy rather than a steady pull through a long period on an inexorable schedule. To be considered, also, is the resentment which arises in a human breast when a man finds himself so completely mastered by a machine.

The public, aware that the automobile industry pays high wages and maintains high factory standards, has been mystified by the degree of heat generated in its labor relations. With all parties in the industry now searching for a comprehensive formula to ensure lasting peace, we believe that a recognition of these strains may perhaps bring a measure of amelioration.—THE EDITORS]

As I walk down the steps with many others, I am disturbed by the thought that the day is only beginning. I suddenly realize in one sensation that there is no escape. It is all unavoidably real and painful. How much energy I must expend to-day has been predetermined by my employer. I try to disregard the thought that is causing this nervous tension which will be with me throughout the hours. Around me I sense a similar reaction. It expresses itself in silence. Men are laughing insincerely. They are ashamed of their emotion. They would rather feel that they were at peace and not a part of this herd who can hide nothing of their day from each other.

The men wander quietly into their places. The shop is beautiful. Machines, blue steel, huge piles of stock. Interesting patterns of windows are darkened by the early hour. This is the impression one gets before he becomes a part of the thing. The beauty is perceivable then. The unbiased observer cannot relate it to the subjective outlook he later acquires.

There is a shrill note. It is impersonal, commanding, and it expresses the entire power which orders the wheels set in motion. The conveyor begins to move immediately. Mysteriously the men are in their places and at work. A man near me grasps the two handles of the air wrench he holds all day long. This is the extent of his operation. He leans forward to each nut as the machine does its work. One nut—two nuts—one motor. It is not necessary for him to change his position. The conveyor brings the next motor to him. One position, one job all day.

Noise is deafening: a roar of machines and the groaning and moaning of hoists; the constant *pssffft-pssffft* of the air hoses. One must shout to be heard. After a time the noise becomes a part of what is natural and goes unnoticed. It merely dulls for the time the particular sense of hearing.

Truss works next to me. We are breaking a man in. There is a lot of experimenting to find out how to divide the jobs so as to achieve the maximum of group efficiency. The job is new to me, too. We are putting fuel connections on the carburetor. Between Truss and me we do three men's work. We cannot keep up. Luckily we know enough not to take it out on each other. We cuss and work in a fit of nervousness. The nut which is supposed to be previously tightened for me won't screw down because it is a bit undersized. I try to tighten it with my fingers, but I keep slipping behind. I am losing my temper. The foreman and relief man have been filling in occasionally for the man who should be there. We just can't do it. Truss snaps out, 'Hell with 'em! Let their damn motors go by if we can't get 'em!' We work and mumble curses. I finally discover how to put my wrench in the hole in such a way as to bite it into the soft brass and twist the lock nut down to where I can get a wrench on it. My ingenuity works out to save my fingers, but to my disgust is merely adding to the possibility of Truss and me doing the job without help.

'Watch your quality to-day, men,' says Sammy, the squat line foreman. We are working so fast I don't see how anyone can think of quality. The old fellow next to me seems to be having trouble keeping up. He is supposed to run in a bolt on a clamp that I straighten and tighten with a hand wrench. When he gets behind I get behind, too. I take his ratchet wrench and do the added operation myself. I do this to two or three motors and give it back. Finally I just keep the wrench and do the added operation myself. I'll get sore each time I'm put behind anyway, so, to guarantee my own peace, I assume the extra work. He looks at me with mild appreciation and I go on feeling that I have big enough shoulders to make it easier for him. At least I'm younger and he's probably quite tired.

Up in the lavatory I usually lean out the window for a breath of fresh air. The out-of-doors smells fresh and free and reminds me how different it was when I could be outside and away from all this overwhelming noise and steel structure. But I can't take more than two or three breaths, for I must hurry back to the call of my stimulated conscience.

Men about me are constantly cursing and talking filth. Something about the monotonous routine breaks down all restraint. The men in most cases have little in common, but they must talk. The work will not absorb the mind of the normal man, so they must think. The feeling of isolation here leads one to the assurance that his confidences will never escape. Truss, without a trace of conscience, speaks of his more intimate relations with his wife. We work on and on with spurts of conversation. Suddenly a man breaks forth with a mighty howl. Others follow. We set up a howling all over the shop. It is a relief, this howling.

II

As the long-anticipated whistle blows for lunch the men burst into the aisles. There is a rule: 'No running.' Some of the men have developed a lunch-hour walk which is hard to distinguish from a run.

I am sitting on the greasy floor of the lunchroom leaning my back against the rail at the head of the stairs. The lunchroom is a great hall with many tables for the men to eat on. At the top of the stairs is a series of cages wide enough for a man to pass through when he rings his clock card. Twenty or thirty clocks are ringing, *ding-dong, ding-dong*, steadily for half an hour before the men go down to work. The floor is black from the dirty shoes. Some men's shoes are so soaked with oil that the surfaces shine and ooze at each step. The general manner of dress is not neat. The average worker probably wears a pair of work pants or old pants and a blue, brown, or black work shirt. Some wear vests. An old vest will protect the shirt and make a man feel dressed. In the cooler weather the whole costume can be covered when leaving the shop. In many cases it is done in such a manner as to create the illusion that the man is dressed much better than he really is. He usually has an old hat which, although it has become worn and dirty from handling, still retains form. An old topcoat then serves to disguise the rest.

In spite of the poorly regulated lives of these men, many gain weight. There are a great number of big massive hulks. This creates the impression of power. But I seldom see a man with a well-proportioned body. Some have a high left shoulder while the right droops. Some have large gnarled hands, the fingers of which fail to respond readily. Many hands lack a finger here and there. Most of the older men have a larger amount of beef in the region of the buttocks than they need. A protruding belly is almost the rule with the men who have been here long. The stomach muscles become relaxed and deformed from standing long hours in one position. I wonder if these men can be healthy. I suspect that they all have some nature of illness. The prevalence of halitosis might be accounted for some way.

Some of these men develop a surprisingly self-important air as though they were not a part of the group. They flaunt their independence. It has had me fooled since I've been here. Their attitude is effective, yet I sense there is something in it that is off color. The place has robbed these men of their true capacities and denied them a life of growth; but it cannot force them to be humble. Their outward front expresses an ownership of all those things they haven't got. They do even the most menial jobs with an air of great responsibility.

III

The shrill whistle blows. Some men start. It works as well as a whip. There is a rustling of clothing, a dropping of feet, and a prayer-like flow of voices as we go down the stairs.

This afternoon I am transferred to the rod department. My job is to weigh one end of the rod and stripe it with paint according to the colors indicated on the scale. There are usually a few piles of rods beside each man. The men figure it looks better to work this way. I take a rod off the pile and throw it on the scale, which is so made that the rod will sit on two pegs. The color is posted on the indicator instead of the weight, so all the operator needs to know is one color from another. I then pick up another rod, and as I take the first one off I put the next one on. While the scale is coming to a rest I paint the small end of the rod in my hand with a stripe corresponding to its weight. No time is lost. One soon gets so he can take a rod off the scale before it comes to a rest and predict where it will stop. As a matter of fact, to paint 5000 rods a day this is almost necessary.

As I am painting the small end of the rod I realize that I am not conscious of what I am doing. My accuracy surprises me. I seldom make a mistake, yet I never have my mind on my work. Perhaps this is why I am able to obtain accuracy, because my subconscious is more capable of this monotony than my personality.

IV

It is soon after lunch. Someone has heard someone who heard someone else say the line was going home at two-thirty. Gradually it becomes a subject of discussion. Karl says to the bearer of the news, 'You wouldn't kid me, would ya? 'Cause that's a dirty trick.' 'Well, I heard a guy ask a foreman,' he said. We all know a foreman doesn't usually know any more than anyone else, yet we wishfully take stock in the rumor. The spirit of some men rises. Two o'clock finally arrives and there is no word yet. Karl curses the fellow who started the rumor. We still have hope, however, because we hate to abandon any chance of such a pleasant anticipation. After two o'clock we lose spirit.

Sometimes my thoughts will not hold me down. I think about all the mean things I have done, and all the things about myself I disrespect. Or I grow angry at some person out of my past. My thoughts go on and torture me. They are thoughts which I am sure are not sane. I try to stop thinking them and find that I don't really want to. I want to think them through until they satisfy me, and hope they will not come back. They do—and the process begins all over again. I cannot think them through to any finality because my work is constantly bringing me back to consciousness. These days and hours are bad. Sometimes I can lick my anxieties and think more objective thoughts. When I have contact with outside interests I can live them through the long hours of the day. Some days I have two or three good topics for thought. Then I am at peace and will postpone each pleasant thought smugly and with anticipation. As a beginner, I would try to think how fast each period of the day would go. This is a hard thing to get any satisfaction from. The day is just so long, and one gets to be as good a time reckoner as a clock.

I find now that I can put my mind to use. I have gained one thing from this hell. I have learned discipline. I can concentrate for an hour on one subject. But my efforts are fast losing direction. I have lost contact with anything to think about.

To-day I am thinking, as usual, depressed thoughts. I have heard these thoughts, some of them, expressed before, but now I am feeling them from dire reality. I have worked long hours this week. Each day I go to work in the dark and leave in the dark. I have not seen daylight since Sunday, and it is Saturday afternoon. I feel strangely unimportant and insignificant. The experiences of the day have exposed my mode of existence in such a way that I see my relative position here too plainly and deeply for my own comfort. I realize how unimportant is personal worth here. When I come in the gate in the morning I throw off my personality and assume a personality which expresses the institution of which I am a part. The only personality expressed here is the personality of the employer, through those authorized to represent him. There is no market for one's personal quality. Any expression of my own individual self beyond the scope of my work is in bad taste.

When a man insinuates here by any action that he is an individual, he is made to feel that he is not only out of place but doing something dishonorable. One feels that even the time he spends in the lavatory is not a privilege but an imposition. He must hurry back because there are no men to spare. After hours on one operation I realize that the only personal thing required of me is just enough consciousness to operate my body as a machine. Any consciousness beyond that is a contribution to my discomfort and maladjustment. I am a unit of labor, and labor is cheap. There is no market or appreciation of my worth except my self-respect. I struggle to keep it. My mood is perhaps a result of a discussion over the bench with Glen. He says, 'No matter whatcha do, they gotcha licked.' It makes me depressed to see him take himself so cheaply. He is convinced of his lack of value here. I feel a sudden wave of fear that I might some day feel exactly as he does.

Some of the men are taking to horseplay. Horseplay among bench workers has less limitation than among line workers. The bosses are not intolerant of horseplay. It is a noticeable fact that they will tolerate it where they will deal severely with serious loafing. As we are working we are unexpectedly interrupted by the foreman. He steps up between Karl and me. While we stop work and look around, he starts slowly to pave the way for what is to be a bawling out. His Swedish accent drawls out:—

'Now listen, fellas. I don't know whether anybody ever tolja this before or whether ya know how it looks from the outside [glides his fingers over the bench in pattern of self-justification], but I'm gonna tell ya now. Now I ain't kickin' on how much work yer gittin' out er how well yer doin' it. Yer gittin' out enough perductchin and yer work's fine; but whatcher doin' is shovin' a whole buncha rods down the bench in a hurry and then gangin' up an' talkin'. Now if any one of those big shots come down 'ere an' see one guy leanin' on the bench like this, another guy over here standin' around, some guys bunched up here, an' everything all goin' ta hell, they wonder what kinda buncha guys they got down here and a hellova man runnin' it. Now I been takin' a lot up there lately an' I ain't been sayin' nothin'.

Now I don't want to be a —— ——, but if I hafta I will. Those guys been comin' down here lately an' I been hearin' about it. They're kickin' an' they got a kick comin'. So—damn it; you fellas work with me an'—damn it I'll work with you, 'cause—well—ya see how it is, doncha? I ain't kickin' about yer work, but what I wancha ta do is—work a little slower if ya hafta and a little steadier.'

V

We start back to work in silence. It leaves a bad taste and we feel as though we really had been falling down on the job. Later we see him making the rounds, so we feel at least it wasn't meant just for us. We slip into some pretty childish ruts sometimes. We are so completely dulled by our work that trivial and boyish pranks amuse us. We cuss and talk filth.

When four-thirty finally arrives we get word that we are working until six. We have all settled into sullen moods. No one has a thing to say. We are grieved at this regular policy of detaining us without consulting us. Karl is working seriously for some time and finally drops back on one foot and bellows: '—damn it! I'm gettin' sick of this stuff. I guess we never will get out of here before daylight.' He grabs the nearest rod and slams it down on the bench. I am mad too, so I egg him on. We take it out on the most faithful man in the department. Later we take to hollering to build up a morale which will help us to lick the last hour. Finally we are walking out, punching our cards. Laughter is now sincere but weary. It is still dark on the outside. I am so dulled that I have gotten here without realizing it. I stop—ponder. I can't think where I parked my car: the morning was so long ago.

V.   RIGHT AND WRONG

In the 1930s, in factories like the one Gene Richard described in the last section, working men and women wrote a new chapter in American labor history. Encouraged by recent federal legislation (especially the Wagner National Labor Relations Act of 1935), they adopted new tactics in pursuit of an ancient goal: securing the right to form labor unions and bargain collectively with their employers. The most controversial of those new tactics was the "sit-down strike," described in the next three selections in this section. What were the characteristic features of the sit-down strike? To what extent was it a product of the Depression? Why was it especially appropriate to an assembly-line method of ·production? Why did working people feel such a sense of excitement about it? Why were employers so appalled by it? Why was it so effective? What similarities do you see between sit-down strikes, and the reaction to them, and the "sit-*ins*" of the 1960s?

The first selection is from Eli Ginzberg and Hyman Berman, The American Worker in the Twentieth Century: A History through Autobiographies *(New York: The Free Press, 1963), 238-40; the second is from Studs Terkel,* Hard Times: An Oral History of the Great Depression *(New York: Pantheon, 1970), 129-33; the third is from* The New Republic, *89 (January 27, 1937), 377-79.*

It was 1:45 A.M. on January 29, 1936.
Upstairs the foreman passed down the lines, his ears cocked for a

114

murmur, for the barest whisper. . . . He was sure getting the jitters lately. But, my God, the company didn't realize how sore these boys were at the rate cut, and you couldn't tell them thickheaded guys in the front office. No, all they'd say was "We hold you accountable for unbroken production in your department." Jesus, was that the way to treat a good loyal company man, threaten to can him if anything went wrong?

The foreman paced slowly past his workmen, his eyes darting in and out of the machines, eager for any betraying gesture. He heard no word, and he saw no gesture. The hands flashed, the backs bent, the arms reached out in monotonous perfection. The foreman went back to his little desk and sat squirming on the smooth-seated swivel chair. He felt profoundly disturbed. Something, he knew, was coming off. But what? For God's sake, what?

It was 1:57 A.M. January 29, 1936.

The tirebuilders worked in smooth frenzy, sweat around their necks, under their arms. The belt clattered, the insufferable racket and din and monotonous clash and uproar went on in steady rhythm. The clock on the south wall, a big plain clock, hesitated, it's minute hand jumped to two. A tirebuilder at the end of the line looked up, saw the hand jump. The foreman was sitting quietly staring at the lines of men working under the vast pools of light. . . .

The tirebuilder at the end of the line gulped. His hands stopped their quick weaving motions. Every man on the line stiffened. All over the vast room, hands hesitated. The foreman saw the falter, felt it instantly. He jumped up, but he stood beside his desk, his eyes darting quickly from one line to another.

This was it, then. But what was happening? Where was it starting? He stood perfectly still, his heart beating furiously, his throat feeling dry, watching the hesitating hands, watching the broken rhythm.

Then the tirebuilder at the end of the line walked three steps to the master safety switch and, drawing a deep breath, he pulled up the heavy wooden handle. With this signal, in perfect synchronization, with the rhythm they had learned in great mass-production industry, the tirebuilders stepped back from their machines.

Instantly, the noise stopped. The whole room lay in perfect silence. The tirebuilders stood in long lines, touching each other, perfectly motionless, deafened by the silence. A moment ago there had been the weaving hands, the revolving wheels, the clanking belt, the moving hooks, the flashing tire tools. Now there was absolute stillness, no motion anywhere, no sound.

Out of the terrifying quiet came the wondering voice of a big tire-builder near the windows: "Jesus Christ, it's like the end of the world."

He broke the spell, the magic moment of stillness. For now his awed words said the same thing to every man, "We done it! We stopped the belt! By God, we done it!" And men began to cheer hysterically, to shout and howl in the fresh silence. Men wrapped long sinewy arms around their neighbors' shoulders, screaming, "We done it! We done it!"

For the first time in history, American mass-production workers had stopped a conveyor belt and halted the inexorable movement of factory machinery.

The foremen . . . retreated. They locked the fire doors and, five minutes later, opened them on demand. They were amazed by the organization of these revolting workmen. After the first hysteria had died down, the confusion disappeared at once. The ringleader, the man who switched the current off, climbed on the foreman's desk and shouted, "O.K., fellows. Now any of you guys here who ain't with us can get the hell out right now. Go home and stay home and don't let's see your yellow-livered face around here again. Anybody want to leave?"

Nobody did. "O.K.," the speaker went on. "Now we got a lot of things to do. First, we got to have a committee to visit other departments, and let's have some volunteers who ain't chicken-livered." The whole truck-tire department wanted to go. The leader picked half a dozen. "You go downstairs and combine with the auto boys' committee and, listen, it's up to you guys to shut this whole god-damned plant down, see?"

"O.K.," the speaker continued quickly. "Now we got to have a committee to police the floor. We don't want no machinery broken we can get blamed for, and we got to keep the place clean. No gamblin' for money either, and absolutely no drinking. We frisk everybody who comes in, for bottles. We don't take nobody's word for it. A couple of drunks would make this sitdown strike look punk."

"Sitdown strike," the crowd repeated. It was a good phrase. The tirebuilders had never heard it before. They liked it. . . .

The factory superintendent's office was a glum place. Every few minutes a new foreman came in, his eyes blazing, his mouth twitching with rage. "I don't know how they found out," the new ones would say. "My God, I had the fire door locked, but all of a sudden, one of them was up there pulling the switch and right away they open the door and this goddamned roving committee comes in and starts to appoint a police committee and pass out union cards, and get them to elect somebody to this here negotiation committee."

Firestone Plant One gradually shut down completely. The departments that didn't actually sitdown and strike were paralyzed by lack of work or materials. The delicate mechanism of mass production was dealt a brutal fatal blow. Engineers had worked for years to synchronize every labor process in the great factory. The most remote departments were dependent on the flow of materials from some other faraway corner of the great plant. But once the line was broken, factory operations came to an uneven, jerking halt.

As dawn came, the day-shift workers lined up at the time-house, punching in their cards. Still dazed with sleep, they stumbled off streetcars, not knowing what had happened inside the walls of the great yellow brick factory. Yet they found out instantly. . . . The new shift came on, and joined the old sitdowners, the veterans, and listened jealously to their bragging tales of how *they* started it, *they* turned off the current. By noon the men who had come to work at dawn were also veterans, able to lord it over the newcomers. . . .

The strikers themselves were surprised and jubilant when they found so little resistance. They owned the factory. Nobody dared say them nay. So they used power carefully. Clean-up squads kept the factory floors shining. The police committee looked darkly at a man who so much as swore. A tirebuilder, leaning on his machine to watch a tong game was warned by every other man on strike, "Watch out. Don't bust nothin'." Abashed sitdowners apologized to the union committee for suggesting poker at a penny limit. By a little after noon, the tire floors were so crowded a man could hardly find a place to sit down. Three shifts were on sitdown duty and men from the fourth shift illicitly sneaked past the gates and came up to get in on the excitement. Runners carried news between the sitdowners and the union hall. So-and-so's wife had called up to say more power to you, stick it out.

The valleys seethed with the story. Women ran, bundled up in old coats, across their front yards, to call on their neighbors and tell them what was going on at Firestone. Little boys boasted in school recess that their Pops were sitting down in the truck-tire department, and other small boys all but burst with envy and rushed home screaming, "Pa, why can't you sit down?"

The Firestone management for twenty-four hours refused even to discuss settlement with the negotiation committee. . . . The second twenty-four hours they began to change their minds.

Still they hesitated. But at the beginning of the third full day of the sitdown, after fifty-three hours, foremen brought terrible news. All of Plant Two was ready to sitdown in sympathy unless there was an immediate settlement. . . .

Murphy sent for the negotiating committee and consigned to hell the opinions of his fellow factory superintendents. It was all very well to talk about a solid employer front, but in the face of something like this, a man had to act quickly or the whole situation would simply blow up in his face. The settlement promised immediate negotiation on the base rate. It offered three hours' pay per day to all workers who had lost time during the sitdown.

When the committee, breathless and excited, brought the news to the men up in the truck-tire department for a vote, they could hardly talk, they were so jubilant. And the strikers were quite beside themselves. They were getting paid, paid, mind you, for sitting down! And the rate would be negotiated. Glory Hallelujah! . . .

The sitdowners marched out singing, and the sound of their voices went everywhere in the valley. The Firestone sitdowners had won! They won! This sitdown business worked.

Bob Stinson

The Sit-Down

"Everybody has to have something they're really sold on. Some people go to church. If I'd had anything I'm really sold on, it's the UAW."

Regularly, he visits the regional headquarters of the United Automobile Workers Union in Flint, Michigan. He's a small-boned man, in specs, sports shirt and a business suit.

"I started working at Fisher Body in 1917 and retired in '62, with 45 and 8/10 years service. Until 1933, no unions, no rules: you were at the mercy of your foreman. I could go to work at seven o'clock in the morning, and at seven fifteen the boss'd come around and say: you could come back at three o'clock. If he preferred somebody else over you, that person would be called back earlier, though you were there longer.

"I left the plant so many nights hostile. If I were a fella big and strong, I think I'd a picked a fight with the first fella I met on the corner. (Laughs.) It was lousy. Degraded. You might call yourself a man if you was on the street, but as soon as you went through the door and punched your card, you was nothing more or less than a robot. Do this, go there, do that. You'd do it.

"We got involved in a strike in Detroit, and we lost the strike. Went back on our knees. That's the way you learn things. I got laid off in the fall of '31. I wasn't told I was blackballed, but I was told there was no more jobs at Fisher Body for me. So I came to Flint and was hired right off the bat. I'm positive my black marks in Detroit followed me later. (Laughs.)

"We had a Black Legion in this town made up of stool pigeons and little bigotty kind of people. They got themselves in good with the management by puttin' the finger on a union organizer. On the same order as the Klan, night riders. Once in a while, a guy'd come in with a black eye. You'd say, 'What happened?' He'd say, 'I was walking along the street and a guy come from behind and knocked me down.'

"The Black Legion later developed into the Flint Alliance. It was supposed to be made up of the good solid citizens, who were terrorized by these outside agitators, who had come in here to take over the plant. They would get schoolkids to sign these cards, housewives. Every shoe salesman downtown would sign these cards. Businessmen would have everyone in the family sign these cards. They contended they had the overwhelming majority of the people of Flint.

"Most people in town was hopin' to hell the thing'd get solved. They had relatives and friends that they knew working in the plant was no bed of roses. They did accept some of this outside agitator stuff that got in the paper. I think anybody who reads this stuff day after day accepts a little bit of it. The great majority of the people was neutral.

"There was fear. You kept your mouth shut when you was in strange company. Every time you put a union button on, you were told to leave the plant. You were fired so fast, it made your head spin.

"We'd meet in an old ramshackley building. No doubt, stool pigeons came. Frenchie was exposed. Somebody got up on the platform and said, 'I know this guy's a stool pigeon, 'cause I gave him information and it passed right from him to the foreman!' They trapped the guy. Nobody touched him. He just walked down the stairs."

He tells of constant betrayals by the AFL International to which they had belonged, and of the subsequent organization of the CIO, led by John L. Lewis.

THE FLINT SIT-DOWN happened Christmas Eve, 1936. I was in Detroit, playing Santa Claus to a couple of small nieces and nephews. When I came back, the second shift* had pulled the plant. It took about five minutes to shut the line down. The foreman was pretty well astonished. (Laughs.)

The boys pulled the switches and asked all the women who was in Cut-and-Sew to go home. They informed the supervisors they could

* The Men who worked from 4:30 P.M. to 12:30 A.M.

stay, if they stayed in their office. They told the plant police they could do their job as long as they didn't interfere with the workers.

We had guys patrol the plant, see that nobody got involved in anything they shouldn't. If anybody got careless with company property—such as sitting on an automobile cushion without putting burlap over it—he was talked to. You couldn't paint a sign on the wall or anything like that. You used bare springs for a bed. 'Cause if you slept on a finished cushion, it was no longer a new cushion.

Governor Murphy said he hoped to God he would never have to use National Guard against people. But if there was damage to property, he would do so. This was right down our alley, because we invited him to the plant and see how well we were taking care of the place.

They'd assign roles to you. When some of the guys at headquarters wanted to tell some of the guys in the plant what was cookin', I carried the message. I was a scavenger, too.

The merchants cooperated. There'd be apples, bushels of potatoes, crates of oranges that was beginnin' to spoil. Some of our members were also little farmers, they come up with a couple of baskets of junk.

The soup kitchen was outside the plant. The women handled all the cooking, outside of one chef who came from New York. He had anywhere from ten to twenty women washing dishes and peeling potatoes in the strike kitchen. Mostly stews, pretty good meals. They were put in containers and hoisted up through the window. The boys in there had their own plates and cups and saucers.

Didn't the guys want a drink now and then . . . ?

That was one of the hard ones. Even though you had strict discipline in there, anybody wanted to climb through the window, you couldn't stop him. He could leave any time he wanted. There was always some of the boys who would take a day off, go out and see how the old woman was doing. When they'd come back in, if somebody didn't search 'em, why, there'd be a pint.

The plant police would start bringin' in some women. That was damn quickly stopped.

We had 'em outnumbered. They may have been anti-union at the time, but it wasn't more than three or four years later before the plant guards' union was organized. I don't blame 'em. They were dependent on their supervisors for jobs just like we were.

Most of the men had their wives and friends come down, and they'd stand inside the window and they'd talk. Find out how the family was. If the union supplied them with enough coal. . . .

We had a ladies' auxiliary. They'd visit the homes of the guys that was in the plant. They would find out if there was any shortage of coal or food. Then they'd maneuver around amongst themselves until they found some place to get a ton of coal. Some of them even put the arm on Consumer Power if there was a possibility of having her power shut off.

Any of the wives try to talk the guys into coming out?

Some of 'em would have foremen come to their homes: "Sorry, your husband was a very good operator. But if he don't get out of the plant and away from the union, he'll never again have a job at General Motors." If this woman was the least bit scared, she'd come down and cry on her husband's shoulder. He'd more than likely get a little disturbed, get a hold of his strike captain. . . . Maybe we'd send a couple of women out there. Sometimes you just had to let 'em go. Because if you kept them in there, they'd worry so damn much over it, that'd start ruinin' the morale of the rest of the guys.

Morale was very high at the time. It started out kinda ugly because the guys were afraid they put their foot in it and all they was gonna do is lose their jobs. But as time went on, they begin to realize they could win this darn thing, 'cause we had a lot of outside people comin' in showin' their sympathy.

Time after time, people would come driving by the plant slowly. They might pull up at the curb and roll down the window and say, "How you guys doin'?" Our guys would be lookin' out the windows, they'd be singin' songs and hollerin'. Just generally keeping themselves alive.

Sometimes a guy'd come up to you on the street and say, "How the guys doin'?" You say, "They're doin' all right." Then he'd give ya a song and dance: "I hear the boys at Chevrolet are gonna get run out tonight."* I'd say, "Hogwash." He'd end with sayin': "Well, I wish you guys the best of luck because, God damn, when I worked there it was a mess." The guy'd turn around and walk away.

Nationally known people contributed to our strike fund. Mrs. Roosevelt for one. We even had a member of Parliament come from England and address us.

Lotta things worked for the union we hadn't even anticipated. Company tried to shut off the heat. It was a bluff. Nobody moved for half an hour, so they turned it back on again. They didn't want the pipes to get cold. (Laughs.) If the heat was allowed to drop, then the pipes will separate—they were all jointed together—and then you got a problem.

Some of the time you were scared, because there was all kinds of rumors going around. We had a sheriff—he came in one night at Fisher One and read the boys the riot act. He told 'em they had to leave. He stood there, looked at 'em a few minutes. A couple of guys began to curse 'im, and he turned around and left himself.

National Guard troops were there. Some from Pontiac, some from Detroit. I lived within a block where they camped. I would pass these young fellas every day. One boy, pretty young, he had a union button on. Was it his union button or was it his dad's? I walked up to him. "Your captain allow you to wear that button?" He says, "I don't know, but I'm gonna find out." (Laughs.) They were twenty-year-olds. Well-behaved boys. No rough stuff, nothing untoward happened.

The men sat in there for forty-four days. Governor Murphy—I get emotional over him (laughs)—was trying to get both sides to meet on some common ground. I think he lost many a good night's sleep. We wouldn't use force. Mr. Knudsen was head of General Motors and, of course, there was John L. Lewis. They'd reach a temporary agree-

* Several other General Motors plants in Flint were the scenes of similar sit-downs. "At Chevrolet Four, there was a knock-down and drag-out fight. That's where the Battle of Bull Run happened. The boys took it over, and the city police and the sheriff's men decided they were gonna throw 'em out. Between the tear gas the police used and the nuts and bolts the strikers used, there was hell to pay. We run 'em off. When the tear gas got in the plant, the women's brigade smashed every damn window they could find to let the air in. It was vicious. (Laughs.) Hans Larson, he was shot in the Battle of Bull Run."

ment and invariably the Flint Alliance or GM headquarters in Detroit would throw a monkey wrench in it. So every morning, Murphy got up with an unsolved problem.

John L. was as close to a Shakespearean actor as any I've ever listened to. He could get up there and damn all the adversaries—he had more command of language. He made a speech that if they shoot the boys out at the plant, they'd have to shoot him first.*

There were a half a dozen false starts at settlement. Finally, we got the word: THE THING IS SETTLED. My God, you had to send about three people, one right after the other, down to some of those plants because the guys didn't believe it. Finally, when they did get it, they marched out of the plants with the flag flyin' and all that stuff.

You'd see some guys comin' out of there with whiskers as long as Santa Claus. They made a rule they wasn't gonna shave until the strike was over. Oh, it was just like—you've gone through the Armistice delirium, haven't you? Everybody was runnin' around shaking everybody by the hand, sayin', "Jesus, you look strange, you got a beard on you now." (Laughs.) Women kissin' their husbands. There was a lotta drunks on the streets that night.

When Mr. Knudsen put his name to a piece of paper and says that General Motors recognizes the UAW-CIO—until that moment, we were non-people, we didn't even exist. (Laughs.) That was the big one. (His eyes are moist.)

THE SIT-DOWN strike is the most important development in the technique of labor disputes in a generation; the strike of the United Automobile Workers against the General Motors Corporation is probably the most significant struggle in American industry since the War. For these among other reasons I came to Flint, heart of the storm, to have a look at what is happening.

---

* When Governor Murphy was being urged to use the National Guard to oust the sit-downers, Lewis orated: "I shall personally enter General Motors' Chevrolet Plant Number Four. I shall order the men to disregard your order, to stand fast. I shall then walk up to the largest window in the plant, open it, divest myself of my outer raiment, remove my shirt and bare my bosom. Then, when you order your troops to fire, mine will be the first breast those bullets will strike. And, as my body falls from the window to the ground, you will listen to the voice of your grandfather as he whispers in your ear, 'Frank, are you sure you are doing the right thing?' "

To get inside a plant while a sit-down is in progress is a hard job. On the day I entered Fisher Body Number One, the strikers had been holding the fort for two weeks. In that time not a soul had entered the building without their consent, and very few under any circumstances. When our car pulled up at the curb before the big, modern structure, set back in a green lawn like a Middle Western high school, a reception committee of five or six sturdy men was waiting. They promptly searched our party, and the car, for weapons. Only when they had been reassured as to our identity were we allowed to go up the walk to the plant itself. All the doors had been shut and heavily barricaded, two weeks earlier. To get in, you climbed on a pile of packing boxes, and swung yourself over the lower third of a heavy window of steel and opaque glass, hinged horizontally at the top. On a platform just inside was another reception committee, friendly enough on the surface but with grim undertones in their voices as they checked over our credentials. During the whole period of the sit-down, nobody left or entered the plant without a pass, and without being searched on his way out and in.

The room in which we found ourselves was a vast oblong, used for building automobile bodies. A double line of these extended the length of the plant, close together, looking with their uniform gray color and their smooth and bulging contours a little like so many kneeling elephants, trunk to tail. As you went forward along the line, each of these bodies was a trifle closer to completion than the one behind it; those at the very end even had the colors they will bear when chassis, engine and wheels have been added and they are off to the road.

Fifteen hundred men had lived for two weeks in a building never intended to be lived in at all, yet the place was remarkably neat and tidy, at least as clean as it is under normal conditions. Beds were made up on the floor of each car, the seats being removed if necessary, and the members of the night shift of guards were sound asleep in the haphazard quarters. They had no weapons of any kind except braided leather billies improvised inside the plant after the sit-down had started. The guards off duty slept in their clothes, with these billies thrust into a pocket or, sometimes, loosely grasped in the sleeper's hand.

The degree of organization among these men was something to

think about. An elected strike committee was in general control. Every man had specified duties, to be performed at specified hours. Meals were prepared with food brought by friends on the outside and passed in through a window, these meals being served in the plant cafeteria at stipulated hours. A barber shop was in operation in one of the rest rooms. Liquor was absolutely forbidden. An emergency post office was set up and there was a heavy movement of mail in both directions—all of it censored by a special committee.

For recreation, the men played cards or listened to the radio, or to a daily concert by the members of the workmen's band, who were staying in. Hundreds of friends and relatives of the strikers visited them every day. With characteristic Yankee ingenuity, the strikers had rigged up a loud-speaker system throughout the plant, with a microphone at the "main entrance." When a visitor called to see any given striker, he was paged over the loud-speaker system. When meetings of all the strikers (except the guards on duty) were held, the union leaders or the members of the strike committee also used a microphone, to make sure of being heard by their listeners, sitting on the floor in the odd bits of space not occupied by machines. I could not see—and I looked for it carefully—the slightest damage done anywhere to any property of the General Motors Corporation. The nearly completed car bodies, for example, were as clean as they would be in the salesroom, their glass and metal shining.

The record of the strikers is a great deal better than that of the city authorities of Flint and of the General Motors Corporation whose eager servants those city authorities have proved to be. A few days before my visit there took place the so-called riot at Fisher Body Number One. I hope the Senate Civil Liberties Committee will investigate that riot. I believe they will find it as disgraceful an incident in American labor relations as we have seen in a long time. Here, in briefest outline, is the story.

For ten days, the sit-down strike had continued with the tacit consent of the General Motors Corporation. Then, on Monday, January 11, these tactics were suddenly changed. The heat in the plant, controlled from an external source, was cut off. Friends of the strikers were refused access to the building for the purpose of bringing food. The main gate of the plant was locked and ladders giving access to the windows were taken away. It was evident that an attempt was being made to force the men out of the building. Late that day, the police blockaded the streets adjacent to the plant. Persons whose cars were parked in the area were brusquely told to go elsewhere. The police assembled in force, with revolvers, gas guns and grenades, loaded with both tear and nauseating gas. The private guards inside the plant, who had heretofore shown no hostility to the strikers, refused to unlock the gates and let food come in. (I might add that when the strikers took away the keys, these guards promptly retired to the ladies' lavatory, locked themselves in, and stayed there, as a result of which the strikers have been charged with kidnaping.) Meanwhile, friends of the strikers had gathered in the streets outside, and when the gates were opened by the sit-downers, the mêlée began. For five hours, the police fought the crowd, with clubs, tear and nauseating gas and revolvers. They shot fourteen people, one of whom may die. Hundreds of others suffered minor injuries or were affected by the gas which, contrary to general opinion, can and often does have extremely serious consequences.

It is a paradox of modern life that the strikers during this medieval struggle should have been aided by such an ultra-modern device as a "sound truck," an automobile equipped with loud speaker and microphone. Throughout the strike this equipment had been used in open-air meetings, in trips through the city to advertise such meetings, and as a means of communication with the sit-down strikers from the outside. During the Battle of Flint the sound truck was on the scene, with Victor Reuther at the microphone. Reuther, with his two brothers, Roy and Walter, is typical of the new leadership that is coming into the American labor movement, young, well educated, the sort of man who could probably make a lot of money if he cared to accept the dominant American pattern as people like Knudsen and Sloan have accepted it. Victor Reuther, from the sound truck, directed the strategy of the strikers, even when the police began shooting at him through the windows of the Chevrolet factory across the street and he was forced to drop to the floor, taking the microphone with him, to avoid being hit. A dramatic incident of the struggle came when a young woman, the wife of a striker (there were many women in the crowd, who got from the police the same treatment the men did), rushed to the truck, took the microphone, told the police what she thought of them and demanded that they stop shooting at the workers, members of their own class.

Throughout the strike, the citizens of Flint have acted as though they were trying to give a model demonstration of the cringing subservience characteristic of public officials in a one-company town. The local newspaper has been 100-percent anti-striker 100 percent of the time. The local broadcasting station has given its facilities to practically anybody on the company's side but has refused to permit the strikers to tell their story. Everybody now knows about Judge Edward D. Black, who issued an injunction against the strikers while himself holding more than 3,600 shares of General Motors stock—an action that stirred even the excessively lethargic American Bar Association. A "Flint Alliance" has been formed, a semi-fascist group along the lines of the vigilante organizations familiar elsewhere in the country. Money has been spent freely for expensive billboard advertising in Flint upholding the so-called "American plan"—which means in a nutshell as little money as possible for the workers and as much as possible for the owners.

While Flint has been the front-line trench of a battle that has included many other cities, all the way from Oakland in the West to Atlanta in the Southeast, the GHQ for the strikers has been the office of the United Auto Workers in Detroit. Here Homer Martin, youthful, pink-cheeked president of the union, sits behind a twenty-dollar oak desk and directs the struggle that means so much, not only to the automobile workers, but to the CIO and to the whole future of American labor. On the day I saw him he had been almost without sleep for forty-eight hours; he had been battling for twelve and fourteen hours at a time with the best brains and the strongest wills money can buy, engaged to defend the corporation; yet he remained calm and low-voiced, sure of ultimate victory and entirely conscious of its significance. It is probably true that if he and John L. Lewis of the CIO had been entirely free to pick their own time and place, the struggle in automobiles would have come somewhat later, might even have been postponed until after a victory had been won in steel or in rubber or in coal. The auto workers' strike was primarily a rank-and-file movement. Whether it will be successful cannot be predicted at the time of this writing. But it has already achieved one or two notable things. It has forced Messrs. Sloan and Knudsen* down off their high horse; they said they would not negotiate, and they did. It has brought about a really amazing sense of solidarity and consciousness of their own strength among the members. Reports of increases in membership were pouring into Detroit over the week-end of January 17—500 in a single day in one town, 800 in another, 700 in a third.

Two chief charges have been made against the union in this strike, in the press of the country. It is said that the UAW represents only a small minority of the workers, many others of whom resent the closing of the plants and are eager to get back to work. It is further said that the sit-down strike is an illegal seizure of property and is, as David Lawrence called it, "extortion." As to the first of these points, Martin flatly claims a majority of all the General Motors employees. He charges that photographs published in Detroit newspapers purporting to show mass meetings of anti-union workers were in fact pictures of men waiting to get their pay checks, many of them pro-union. I do not know the exact facts about the matter, but I do know this: that no worker wants longer hours and smaller pay when he can get shorter hours and more money. If the union brings these things, all but a minute and crabbed minority will support the organization. I have been watching labor struggles for a third of a century, and I have never yet seen the cry about the poor working man who is coerced by the union come from anybody except those who want to see the working man coerced by the employer. As to whether the sit-down strike constitutes extortion, I might get more excited about this if I did not remember so many instances of extortion on the other side. It is extortion when men are locked out and permitted to come back to work only at starvation wages. It is extortion when they are speeded up very nearly to the breaking point. It is extortion when state authorities send soldiers and police against them with tear gas, clubs and bullets.

In Great Britain, I am informed, the sort of thing that has been happening in Flint would be almost impossible because British employers learned years ago that the way to get on with labor is to encourage strong, responsibly led labor unions, representative of the

* William S. Knudsen and Alfred P. Sloan, vice-president and President, respectively, of General Motors.

entire body of workers, and to make with them agreements that will be respected because they are respectable. Fifteen years hence, I have no doubt that collective bargaining will be an established fact throughout American mass industry, bargaining on behalf of the workers as a whole and not on behalf of little groups of highly skilled craftsmen who are now protected—so to speak—by the silver-haired leaders of the A.F. of L. When that day comes, I do not doubt that what happened in Flint last week will seem as remote—and as inexplicable—as the French and Indian wars.

Flint, Michigan.   BRUCE BLIVEN.

Comment on the sit-down strikes in the 1930s was hotly divided. Almost all observers saw great principles of law and morality at stake, and most commentators were admitted partisans of either labor or management. The following two selections are typical of the debate over sit-downs, and over the status of labor in general. The first selection, an editorial from *The New Republic*, favors the strikers, while the second, from a speech by Congressman Martin Dies (Democrat, Texas) condemns them. What are their principal points of disagreement? Were the strikes illegal? Were they immoral? Were they a threat to property? What is Congressman Dies' attitude toward property? Would similar action provoke the same debate today? Has the moral climate, with regard to the labor movement, changed since the 1930s? Why?

The first selection is from The New Republic, *89 (February 3, 1937), 398; the second is from a speech by Martin Dies in the House of Representatives, March 23, 1937 (Congressional Record, 75th Congress, First Session, pp. 2637-39).*

The point to remember is that General Motors, the Wall Street forces that stand behind General Motors and, indeed, big industry and ownership throughout the country, are all just as bitterly anti-union as they ever were. As several people have recently pointed out, American business is at least a generation behind our British cousins in this regard. The British have learned over many years that the way to get along with labor is to encourage strong, comprehensive and ably led unions and to negotiate with them in a reasonable spirit. What General Motors and similar firms in this country actually want is no unions at all. If they can't have that, they want company unions, which only pretend to serve the workers' interests. Whenever a real union appears, they do their best to break it up by sending in spies and saboteurs and by firing and blacklisting the leaders.

The reaction to Mr. John L. Lewis' request for administration support, last week, must be looked at in the light of the foregoing facts. It is quite true that his impromptu remark came at a moment when it embarrassed the President and was therefore indiscreet, though its indiscretion hardly justified Mr. Roosevelt's sharp comment a few hours later. It is obvious that the President of the United States must not personally intervene in a serious strike unless and until it is perfectly sure that his intervention will be successful. For him to try and fail would not only be an unendurable blow to his prestige, but would be followed by an extremely ugly situation. Mr. Roosevelt has already 'intervened' in the strike indirectly, through Miss Perkins, Mr. Grady and Governor Murphy.

While we agree that Mr. Lewis was tactless, we do not agree with the storm of angry comment on his action that was witnessed in the American press. Most of that comment has come from newspapers that were anti-union anyhow and were looking for every possible excuse to attack the workers. The fact that the General Motors Corporation is one of the country's largest advertisers, spending many millions annually to buy space in newspapers and magazines, does not make the attitude of the press any prettier.

For the fact remains that Mr. Lewis is right and what he said was true. The President has time and time again pledged himself and his administration to support genuine collective bargaining. That support has been written into one piece of legislation after another, from the NRA to the National Labor Relations Act. It is a cornerstone of the entire New Deal. It is unthinkable that it should now be abandoned. The only question is how it shall be applied, and the only right answer is, through a genuine union representative of the genuine desires of the workers.

The same press that jumped on Mr. Lewis so gleefully is continuing to argue that the United Automobile Workers represent only a minority of the employees of General Motors. We see no reason to doubt Mr. Homer Martin's repudiation of this charge, but even if it were true, we still think the course of justice and common sense would be to deal with the union as spokesman for all the workers. Is America's memory so short that we have already forgotten the dismal experience of the President's agreement in the automobile industry? That agreement was an attempt to do exactly what Messrs. Sloan and Knudsen now propose: to give representation to every group, large or small, genuine or fake, that called itself a union. It was an abject failure which broke down before it was even under way. What earthly reason is there now for making the same mistake again?

Much is being heard of the illegality of the sit-down strike, and there are brave words about rushing through a Supreme Court decision forbidding such things. Writers like David Lawrence and George Sokolsky discuss the strike as though the men who are staying in were an invading army, determined to destroy the plants for all time, instead of being workers just as anxious to get back to their jobs as anyone is to have them do so. The debate over legality seems to us entirely off the point. The real objection to the sit-down is that it is effective; the employers are willing to grant to labor any weapon except one that works. It is perfectly plain that General Motors' objection to the sit-down is that they don't want to settle with the union.

In all this cloud of words, it is as well to stick to first principles: the best status for industry is genuine collective bargaining. The attempt to bring this about through a multitude of weak unions has never worked and never will. The UAW is the strongest and most ably led union the automobile industry has ever seen. The obvious sensible course is for the industry to come to terms with it, and get back to work.

* * *

Because some captains of industry and finance have employed lawless and indefensible methods to achieve their greedy objectives does not justify labor in doing the same thing. In fact, a consideration of the consequences which these captains of high finance and industry brought upon themselves and upon others should act as an object lesson to deter labor from committing the same outrages. For, by such lawlessness, capital lost the support and confidence of the public and, by the same methods, labor is likely to suffer the same consequences.

It was under the auspicious union of liberty and order that we grew to be a great republic. The two go hand in hand—they are like Siamese twins who have a common vertebra. To sever order from liberty is to produce the instant death of both. What would the laboring man, who has seized the plant of his employer and refuses to permit him to enter, say if he went home at night and found someone in possession of his home or his automobile in violation of law? Would he not cry out for immediate redress at the hands of the court? The principle is the same in both instances, and if he expects protection in the enjoyment of his home and earnings, then he must be willing to accord the same rights to his employer.

I would be the first man to insist upon the right of labor to strike, to picket, and to pursue any other lawful means to secure a redress of wrongs and to obtain its just dues, but there is a vast difference between the right of labor to strike and their right to seize possession of other peoples' property and to refuse to give up possession until their demands are met.

There is a world of difference between the refusal to work and the refusal to permit the owners of property to enter it and have access to their own files and offices. There is a marked distinction between the right of labor to picket and their right to surround the courthouses and seek to interfere with the orderly administration of justice. For the pure and impartial administration of justice is the greatest bulwark of freedom in America and is indispensable to the very existence of free government. So while I would be the first man to defend the right of labor to strike, I am just as vigorously opposed to the unlawful use of the property which belongs to others. Between the right to strike and the right to continue a so-called sit-down strike there is a chasm as wide as the ocean itself which can never be spanned by constitutional and democratic methods.

As one who has been the unfailing friend of labor in its honest aspirations to better its lot—as one who has consistently supported measures designed to eliminate with child-labor and sweatshop conditions and to give to labor the right of collective bargaining and to improve the standards of work and pay among the laboring people—as one who has consistently voted for all legislation to curb the lawlessness in the business and financial world and to restrain the greed and selfishness that prevailed—as one who championed the cause of organized labor at a time when there was only a handful of members in my district and when it was unpopular to take such a stand, I denounce this lawlessness as un-American and inimical to the best interests of our country. I yield to no man in my loyalty to the cause of honest and deserving labor, but I do know and I do declare that if sit-down strikes succeed America will fail. If there ever was a time when those in places of authority, whether under municipal, State, or Federal government, should speak out in clear and unmistakable language, it is now. Let those who are responsible for this form of lawlessness realize that they stand before the bar of public opinion with the condemnation and disapproval of every thinking American citizen and of every public official who has the true cause of labor at heart.

VI. HEAVEN AND EARTH

From the days of the Puritans, through the time of the religious revivals of the early eighteenth and nineteenth centuries, down even to the school-prayer controversy of the present day, America has been considered a religious country. Yet many observers in the 1930s noticed that the Depression—the kind of affliction that had turned men to God and the churches in the past—seemed to stimulate no increase in religious devotion among the American people. Both the following selections comment on this apparent curiosity. How do they explain it? How had America become such a secular society in the twentieth century? Was it the character of the Depression, or the character of the American people in the 1930s, that discouraged them from responding to the crisis in religious terms? If God or the devil was not to blame, who was? If the victims of the Depression did not turn to religion for comfort, where did they turn?

The first selection is from Robert S. Lynd and Helen Merrell Lynd, Middletown in Transition: A Study in Cultural Conflict *(New York: Harcourt, Brace and Co., 1937), 301-03; the second is from* The Christian Century, *52 (September 18, 1935), 1168-70.*

Since the outward forms of religion are seemingly so unchanged, as much effort as possible was made within the time available to discover whether the depression has affected the inner feeling of Middletown people as regards religion. Have they been turning privately, if not publicly, to religion with greater frequency and depth of devotion? That those closest to local religious life have hoped for some such change is suggested by the following statement which served as the keynote to a Middletown rally of Sunday-school superintendents in 1932: "A great religious awakening follows each depression: What are we going to do about it? How can we increase attendance and develop leadership for Sunday school and mission work?" The very raising of these questions as relating to a future event suggests, perhaps, that there had been no marked upsurge up to that time. The following comments to the investigator in 1935 serve to answer the question further:

Comment by a thoughtful minister, an exceptionally dis-criminating religious leader of some ten years' local residence: "The depression has brought a resurgence of earnest religious fund-amentalism among the weaker working-class sects on the South Side—probably due in part to the number of casual workers that have drifted in from the Southern Mountains—but the uptown church-es have seen little similar revival of interest."

Comment by the energetic pastor of one of the larger working-class churches, associated with one of the large denominations: "There has been some turning to religion during the depression, but it has been very slight and not permanent. Despite my constant visit-ing and an annual survey I make of all families in my district, there has been very little increase in church attendance and even less in-crease in religious interest on the South Side. There has been no in-crease at all in the children's interest."

Comment by the minister of one of the smaller and more primitive sects composed entirely of working-class people: "There has been only a very small turning to religion during the depression. My church has grown from 40 to 200 during the past four or five years as it is one of only two churches of our denomination and draws working people from all over the city. Our people live in great uncer-tainty as to whether they'll be working next week. There hasn't been much deepening of their aims and values except that their aims have shortened because of their constant economic uncertainty. I expect that when prosperity returns people will probably turn away from the church again—just as the Old Testament predicts."

Comment by an unemployed factory worker: "I and a few other men I know have got interested in going to church because we didn't have any money to go anywhere else. Then we got interested in the teachings and activities and stuck. I guess we'll drift away again when things pick up."

Comment by another workingman: "I don't go to church because the church ought to have something to meet the needs of laboring men, and the laborers feel that the administration of churches is in the hands of wealth."

A physician closely in touch with many phases of Middletown life seemed to sum up the situation with considerable accuracy when he said:

"There is no wave of religious feeling in [Middletown] in the depression, despite the prediction of the ministerial profession that the depression would bring the people closer to God. The churches, although they constantly point to their yearly membership growth, are conscious of the fact that they are slowly slipping. The average [Middletown] citizen has very definite religious beliefs, but for the most part they are a kind of automatic part of the scheme of inherited things and not anything he uses particularly in his daily life. And the depression hasn't changed this."

It is possibly indicative of the apparently negligible effect of the depression as a quickening factor in local religious life that the bottom has dropped out of the revival movement which flourished in 1925; though other social changes are undoubtedly operative here also. According to a prominent minister: "The business-class churches are slowly giving up the revival idea. The last one, tried as a union effort in the spring of 1930, almost died on our hands. We used the big high-school basketball auditorium. The revival was billed as a great drive to regenerate Middletown. Toward the end of the four weeks it became very difficult to get attendance. I don't think these churches have much stomach for trying it again." There has been a meager sprinkling of revivals in individual working-class churches during the depression, with the usual meetings "for men only" at which the revivalist speaks on "the trio of evils—women, wine, and gambling," while his wife talks to the women on "Why you should not get a divorce." In August, 1935, a girl evangelist "who has been preaching since she was 14" conducted a revival in a working-class church with the aid of a director of music who "was once leading tenor in the Boston Grand Opera Company . . . where he sang leading roles in *Il Trovatore* and *The Bohemian Girl.*" The evangelist's sermon subjects included "Thrills," "Choosing Sides," "The First Mortgage," "Beyond Sunset," "America's Greatest Need," "Evolution—Man or Monkey?" Such a series of meetings still arouses some response in a working-class church. *But, on the whole, if the number of revivals is any index of religious interest in the depression, there has been a marked recession.*

WHY NO REVIVAL?

It must be a subject of at least occasional reflection on the part of thoughtful people that this period of depression has brought forth no revival of religion. We are accustomed to expect revivals in such periods. They have regularly come in the past, and from the beginning of the present depression a revival has been persistently predicted, particularly by those who are in some special sense charged with a professional responsiblity for what is called evangelism. Dr. Charles L. Goodell, representing the commission on evangelism of the Federal council of churches, was quoted by a Christian Century correspondent recently as having said: "Every period of depression is marked by a spiritual aspiration and followed by a great yearning." In reply to the question, Are there signs of an approaching revival? Dr. Goodell said that he was hopeful and pointed to certain evidences upon which his hope was based, among which was a new seriousness on the part of college students.

There can be no doubt of the changing mood of youth, as also of their elders, and that this change points strongly in the direction of religion. But great care must be exercised not to interpret this mood as a foretoken of the return of that institution which our Protestant

evangelicalism designates by the word "revival." If there are signs of
its return such signs are to be regarded not with gladness but with
foreboding. Those whose memories go back to the pre-war period
cannot forget the spiritual devastation wrought by the "revival cam-
paigns" which swept through the churches. Surely there is none
among us who would wish for the return of the high-pressure, bla-
tant, mercenary, sensation-seeking revival of those years. That kind
of revival is not an expression of vital religion but of the lack of it.

The revival is one thing, and the revival of religion is something
else. There are reasons for expecting that concerted efforts will be
made in the near future to revive the revival, and the churches will
need to be on their guard against them. But for the revival of religion
all devout souls earnestly and persistently pray. Dr. Goodell's use of
the changing attitude of college students as a promising sign of
religious revival is thoroughly sound. There can be no doubt that
there is in the colleges a general deflation of the humanistic spirit of
self-sufficiency which developed to inordinate dimensions in the
prosperity of the first post-war decade. The depression has provided
the basic condition for this change of mood. But there are other fac-
tors in this change, among which is the converging thought of the
most commanding minds in science and philosophy upon the conception of God. Materialism as a philosophy is dead. And it is getting so
that it is no longer "smart" to be an atheist.

All this may be true and prophetic, but those of us who believe
that the Christian church is of the essence of Christianity, cannot
help inquiring whether or not this new mood of wistfulness is turning
toward the church as the true and most nearly adequate instrument
through which to express its inchoate faith. When this question is
put, it must be confessed that there are not yet any convincing signs
of religious revival. The current depression has lasted longer than
any previous one, and despite the President's optimistic reference to
it as the "recent" depression, it bids fair to remain with us for a long
time yet. But despite the unprecedented length of the depression, and
despite the evidences of a new spiritual mood on the part of both
youth and its elders, there is no mass movement of the people toward
the churches.

We might as well be frank about it. This depression has lasted too
long for Christian leaders to continue to assert that because religion

has always experienced revival in past depressions we are sure even yet to witness a like phenomenon in this. That is mere wishful talk. Unless it is accompanied by a critical analysis of present conditions, it may bring a false complacency. It also raises apprehension lest our leaders may encourage false forms of revivalism and so block the way to true and deep religious revival. The better course is to admit candidly that there are as yet no clear signs of the kind of revival that grows out of the sympathetic contact of the church with the general community. Having made this admission, the candid mind will ask why it is so. The answer may be a dismal one. On the other hand, it may be far more encouraging than mere blind whipping up of morale.

The fact that the present period of economic breakdown, accompanied by unemployment on so vast a scale that the government is compelled to provide the livelihood of 20 per cent of the total population, has not registered itself in an increased popular attendance at the churches and a more intense devotion to the corporate expression of moral guilt and spiritual need, ought to give pause to our uncritical optimism and send us thoughtfully to reconsider the situation. If we do so, we shall discover that there is a basic psychology in the present depression which has not characterized previous ones, and that this accounts for the absence of a religious reaction to the experiences people are living through.

In former economic calamities, men have tended to regard their suffering as due to forces beyond their control. Hard times sprang mysteriously out of the nature of things. This was obviously true in agricultural societies in which prosperity depended directly on rain and sun and soil, that is, much more upon God than upon man. But up to now, it has been hardly less true of industrial societies. The economic order has generally been regarded as virtually a part of the cosmic order, and a calamity arising within it was felt to be as inexorable as drought or flood or storm in nature. Economics was a part of nature, in the sense that as nature must, for the most part, be accepted for what she is and does, so the operation of "economic law" must be accepted. The religious attitude toward such an inexorable situation was, therefore, one of awe and resignation, accompanied by the consciousness that, no doubt, men had offended God and that only by repentance could God be reconciled. It was this belief and mood which underlay all religious revivals in previous depressions. Men in their helplessness were driven by calamity to seek help from God and to make their peace with him.

But in this depression it is different. The idea is now abroad that so-called economic law is not like the laws of nature. We are no longer under the illusion that our economic system is fixed for us. Among the masses of men, as well as the more sophisticated, the idea prevails that our economic system is a man-made system. And being man-made it can be remade. There are many theories as to how it can be remade, but men are conscious, as they never were in any previous depression, that this depression is unnecessary. It is not an "act of God," like an earthquake, but is due to the failure of human intelligence or the blind power of entrenched privilege, or both. It is therefore not something about which one need get "religious." What one needs is to become intelligent, rather than religious, and to help unify the power of the unprivileged masses for the setting up of an economic system whose productive processes shall function for human use, not for the profits of a single class.

Obviously, a society in this mood is not likely to flock to the churches on account of the depression. It may have other reasons for going to the churches, but the depression provides no special reasons. It does not occur to the people that religion could have any relation to their social unintelligence, or to the selfishness and perversity of those who sit in privileged places. And even more remote from their thought is the possibility that religion may be requisite both in securing the more just and rational social order which they demand and in stabilizing it when once it is attained. Religion, the people have been taught, has nothing inherently to do with these social and economic matters. Religion is a very personal, private thing. It belongs to the "inner life" and to the cosmic order, but is not applicable to the realm of social relationships which lies between the two.

A revival of religion which can have any relevancy to the depression must take account of this popular attitude. But the truth is that the Christian church has come into this depression wholly unprepared to take account of it, and to minister to the deepest human need which it discloses. The organized church is unable to interpret the new mood. Its traditional ministry to personal need does not apply here. It has no insight nor technique for interpreting the modern social mood as something *religious*, and for capitalizing it on behalf of religion. If, then, we would canvass all possible quarters for signs of religious revival, we must look inside the Christian church, as well as to the general temper of the time. The question to ask is: Are there signs that the Christian church is becoming alive to the essentially religious nature of the social problem which mankind now confronts? We believe that there are enormously important tokens of such an awakening. But we shall be able to discern them only if we understand why the church has been unready to meet its new responsibilities. There are three reasons why the church came into this situation unprepared to minister to it.

One reason is that Protestant evangelicalism has never developed an awareness of the possibility of repentance for social or corporate evil. Repentance unto salvation, in our churches, has been confined to private sins and to transcendental sin. These are the subject matter of evangelical revivalism. Never has our Protestantism found the way, or felt the need, or conceived the possibility of bringing the corporate evil of the social order to the altar and there expiating it in contrition and repentance before God. Suppose that the church had come into this depression with a tested technique for dealing with social sin, with an established habit of prophetic preaching in this realm, and with a known record of sympathy with the unprivileged masses, would we not have seen a revival of religion in this period?

A second reason why our spiritual renewal is delayed in these times of profound human need, is that Protestantism has always tended to assume—following Luther's tragic example—that God is on the side of the established order, and that the church also must be on that side. It is such an easy fallacy for religion to fall into: to assume that God is a kind of super-policeman concerned with *order*, as such, and that he is always against any innovation whose coming must cause disorder. The effect of this fallacy in the church's thinking is tragic. It means that the masses of mankind think that God goes when a particular economic order goes! Does not the history of Christianity teach us that God is always on the side of minorities, and that the emergence of a new social order is more likely to mean that God is coming rather than that he is going? By allowing it to be assumed that God is on the side of the status quo, the church has been rendered unable to speak with full prophetic authority in an hour like the present when the social order is undergoing radical reconstruction.

Finally, it must be confessed that Protestantism, long identified with the capitalistic system, champion of moral virtues themselves derived from capitalism rather than from the teaching of Jesus, and subsidized for so long by the alms and philanthropies of capitalistic wealth—this Protestant church is itself confused, because it, too, is caught in the same revolutionary change which the social order is undergoing. How can the blind lead the blind? Is the church which has been so long blind to its responsibility for the character of the social order, now beginning to see? There are favorable signs; the church is at least able to see men as trees walking. The social gospel is steadily making its way into the intelligence and conscience of Christianity's leaders. Its progress may be measured by the fact that there are already thousands of ministers who consider the revivalism of the past with disillusionment and distinct recoil. They have not yet found a fully effective technique nor an adequate content for the gospel of the corporate life, but their competency and insight grow with each added year of study, experiment and communion with Christ.

The situation in which the Christian church now finds itself is one of unreadiness for a revival of religion. But the tokens are too numerous to doubt that it is putting its own house in order. It bends under the judgment which always begins at the house of God. As our evangelists have always taught, but in a sense infinitely more profound than they dreamed, not until this judgment registers can there be a revival of religion.

All of this means, of course, that the blessed revival is actually under way, though the signs are not the conventional ones. True, there is no outpouring as yet; no freshet of grace; no tidal movement. But far up in the creeks and inlets of the church's devotion and intelligence there are gathering the waters of divine revival. At such an hour as we think not, the tide will turn, and come in—silent, irresistible, and full.

Yet on the other hand, religious life in America went on, often seeking new forms to accommodate the social changes taking place around the churches. What was new and what was old about the brand of Christianity revealed in the following documents? What role did social class distinctions play in religious life? Did the religious change their tactics to combat the Depression? Were they successful?

From Studs Terkel, Hard Times: An Oral History of the Great Depression *(New York Pantheon: 1970), pp. 165-67, 328-332.*

WIN STRACKE

A Chicago balladeer. Founder of the Old Town School of Folk Music.

I was a soloist at the Fourth Presbyterian Church from '33 to '40. The parishioners were very well-to-do people, whose families had come from New England to Chicago many years ago. I was just beginning to wake up to the fact that there was such a thing as politics and influences in our society. I hadn't really been conscious of a sort of class distinction between the supporters of Alf Landon and the supporters of Roosevelt.

I remember very clearly the Sunday morning before the election of '36. When I got up to sing my solo part at the services, I looked out over the congregation, about nine hundred or a thousand, and it was one sea of yellow. Everybody was decorated with large yellow Landon sunflower buttons. Just the impact of the thing suddenly made me realize there is such a thing as class distinction in America.

The pillar of another church, where I had previously sung, was a very wealthy Chicago industrialist. Great deference was paid to him. At one evening service, he gave a sermon. This was about 1933, in the depths of the Depression, and there was a lot of political protest around. He got up and said that he had searched the Bible from cover to cover and he could not find a single word or sentence or phrase to indicate that Jesus was against capitalism. (Laughs.)

In 1937, '38, I was working with an octet at the Old Heidelberg. We were infuriated because the waiters would stand around reading the *Völkischer Beobachter*, the official Nazi paper. It had been a traditional practice, when a customer had a birthday, they would send up a bottle of Rhine wine—the sommelier would bring up a tray and proceed to pour a glass for every member of the octet. I would say, "We're very happy to salute Mrs. So-and-So," or whoever it was. Then we'd hold up our glasses and sing "*Soll Er Lieber*."

A couple of us said: Ah, the hell with drinking this Rhine wine. So we announced to the headwaiter: no more Rhine wine. The management was furious. We said, "If you don't like it, we'll quit." So we finally settled on the idea that they'd serve us Cuba Libras. From then on, we saluted birthday guests with Cuba Libras. (Laughs.)

I still had my job at the church. So I'd do the first show in my costume: a red jacket, white pants and long Prussian boots. Of course, we had those little pepperbox hats. Heidelberg cadets. I'd sneak in the back way of the Fourth Presbyterian, put a robe over my Heidelberg outfit and sing sacred songs. (Laughs.)

In the Depression, the business of being a singer had lots of hardships. We were all hurting for dough. During one job, a once-a-week radio broadcast, our compensation was a room in the Allerton Hotel. The idea being: if we showed enough initiative, we'd rent the room and thus have compensation for our singing. I was never able to rent my room. The hotel was only about thirty percent occupied, so they weren't giving anything away.

We had one sponsor of a Sunday morning radio program, who owned cemetery lots. We sang old-fashioned hymns and talked about the memorial park. We were paid fifteen bucks apiece. He persuaded us to make recordings, so he could save money. Somehow the old codger talked us into taking, not money, but cemetery lots. I still have seven of them. (Laughs.)

In 1939 I was a chorus member of WGN's "Theater of the Air." I saw and heard Colonel McCormick every Saturday night. There was a ten-minute segment where he'd expound on the defense of Detroit against the Canadians or how he first observed artillery from a balloon at the Battle of Chantigny.

One time I remember he was sitting on the aisle. Next to him was his wife, next to her was his Great Dane, and next to the Great Dane was (laughs) Governor Dwight Green. When the Colonel began his speech, the dog started to snuffle loudly. The Colonel's wife reached over into the Governor's breast pocket, took out his handkerchief and held it over the dog's muzzle. After the talk, she just reached over, put it back in the Governor's pocket. (Laughs.)

In 1940, I was fired by the Fourth Presbyterian Church. I had become active, singing for various causes. I hadn't gotten too much static from this because they were worlds apart. The farm equipment workers were on strike against the McCormick Works. First time since the Haymarket affair. I sang at the union hall. During the evening a film was shown by a local finance company: how strikers could borrow money, during the emergency, and repay it, with interest.

I had heard the minister of the church had been visited by a woman, complaining of my activity. I received a letter from the chairman of the music committee, a member of an old Chicago family, saying my services were no longer required.

The funny thing about it is this man was head of the finance company whose film was shown. So my conclusion was: It's all right to loan money to strikers at interest, but don't sing for 'em for nothing. (Laughs.)

Before my last service, the minister took me up to his study and prayed for me. He asked the Lord to give me guidance, to straighten me out. After the prayer, he strongly suggested I leave town and change my name.

CLAUDE WILLIAMS

His resemblance to the poet, Ezra Pound, is startling.

"I've been run out of the best communities, fired from the best churches and flogged by the best citizens of the South."

He was born and raised in the hills of western Tennessee, "so far back in the sticks they had to pump in daylight to make morning." He began as a fundamentalist, preaching "to save their never-dying, ever-precious souls from the devil's hell eternal." He drilled himself in chapter and verse.

After four years in the town of Lebanon, as an evangelist, he was invited to the Vanderbilt School of Religion. It was a seminar for rural preachers. The teacher who most influenced him referred to Jesus as Son of Man—"he cleared the debris of theological crap and let Him rise among us as a challenging human leader."

I ASSUMED the pastorate of a Presbyterian church in Rome, Tennessee. I took as my text: "Go ye into the world and preach the gospel to every nation." We must treat everybody as persons. An elder said to me that night at dinner: "Preacher, do you mean that damn burrhead is as good as I am?" I answered, "No, but I mean to tell you he's as good as I am." So I had to find another pulpit.

At Auburntown, I said, "Friends, I've enjoyed this pastorate and the people, but I must tell you I think of God as a social being. The Son of Man is worthy of discipleship and the Bible is a revealing book of right and wrong." After that revival meeting, I had to find somewhere else to go.

I come to grief because of a trip I made to Waveland, Mississippi. In 1928. An interracial meeting. I was together with black people for the first time in my life. At the table I was aware of food sticking in my throat before swallowing it. A friend taught me to emphasize the "e" in Negro—to avoid old terms like "nigra," "uncle" and "auntie." I went down to preach to a black church. There were some whites sitting to one side. As the people came out, an old black man was the first I shook hands with. This was in violation of all my upbringing.

I was recommended to a little church in Paris, Arkansas. It was a coal-mining town. They were trying to organize against all odds. We staged a strike and won. As soon's it happened, I began to get money from Moscow. (Laughs.) But I learned this "money from Moscow" spent quicker and bought less than scrip coupons at a plantation robbersary—that's the real name for commissary.

Miners began to come around, from as far as thirty miles. They built the thing with their own hands. We thought of building a proletarian church and a labor temple. I canceled my insurance policies to buy the cement for the foundation—they quit paying my salary. From fifteen active members, we now had over a hundred. One of the elders, a merchant, was furious. "You've got these cantankerous miners—these blatherskites." They accused me of Red-ism and corrupting the minds of the youth. I lost my church. The presbytery met and "dissolved the relationship of the Reverend Claude Williams and the church for the good of the Kingdom of Heaven."

We went down to the town theater for Sunday services. It was filled. Many young people, miners and unemployed. This was '32,

'33. Black people were coming to my home for conferences. Someone said, "You ought to pull the shades down." I said, "No, I want to pull the shades up and let the hypocrites see brotherhood being practiced." I was pretty rash.

The church was $2200 behind in my salary. I refused to leave the manse. They evicted me and sued me for the interest on the money they owed me. One official was the editor of the local paper, the Paris *Express*. We called it the Paris *Excuse*. One was an insurance salesman and another was a retired colonel, who painted his house red, white and blue. So I was driven out and went to Fort Smith.

We staged a hunger march, a thousand or more. The Mayor sent word: The march won't be held. I sent word back: This is America. The march will be held. He said, "We'll turn the hose on you." I said, "You do your duty, and I'll do mine." While we were in the opening prayer, they swarmed down on us. A lot of us landed in jail. The vigilantes were on me pretty regularly. So in the spring of '35, I went to Little Rock.

I worked with black and white unemployed. And taught at the first school of the Southern Tenant Farmers Union. In June of '36, I went to Memphis to prepare a funeral for a black sharecropper who had been beaten to death. His body disappeared. I went to investigate.

Before we got to Earle, Arkansas, five deputies were waiting for us. They took me out of the car. They got me down, four men held me down. This man had a little four-inch leather strop. He was a master. He gave me about sixteen licks. The woman with me kept count. They made a jelly out of me. Then they said, "Let's get some of that fat woman's butt." They applied the lash to her—five or six licks. They were careful not to damage her hose, as they led her through the barbed wire. They didn't know whether to dump me in the river or let me loose. They made me sign a statement that I hadn't been hurt. When I refused, they said, "If you're not through, we're not." I signed. They couldn't use it because it was an admission that they'd had me. They took me to Highway 70 and headed me for Birmingham. A car followed me for miles. I got away from 'em at Brinkley.

That was my real induction. I learned it's one thing to preach radical from the pulpit—people will come to atone for their wrongs by enduring a radical sermon—but when you identify with the people in their battle that's when "you get your money from Moscow." I've been in this fight for forty years. I've spent many a night behind the barbed-wire fence.

"I was defrocked in 1934. But in '42, the Presbyterian people asked me to go to Detroit because of so many southerners there in the auto plants. The established church couldn't reach 'em. I was to be industrial chaplain. They wanted me to put my feet on the desk and get a $5,000 expense account. But I got there out among the people. That's when the presbytery people began to get complaints. G.L.K. Smith and Carl McIntyre and some of the others put so many pressures on, they fired me.

"I returned to the South and continued my work in Birmingham. They preferred charges against me for heresy. It was confirmed by the Presbyterian General Assembly. I returned to Detroit and was ordained in a Negro church."

I've used the Bible as a workingman's book. You'll find the prophets—Moses, Amos, Isaiah and the Son of Man, Old Testament and New—you'll find they were fighting for justice and freedom. On the other side, you find the Pharaohs, the Pilates, the Herods, and the people in the summer houses and the winter houses. These people like John the Baptist are our people and speak our word, but they've been kidnapped by the others and alien words put in their mouth to make us find what they want us to find. Our word is our sword.

I interpreted this for the sharecroppers. We had to meet in little churches, white and black. It was in the tradition of the old underground railway. I translated the Bible from the vertical to the horizontal. How can I reach this man and not further confuse him? He had only one book, the Bible. This had to be the book of rights and wrongs. True religion put to work for the fraternity of all people. All passages in the Book that could be used to further this day I underlined in red pencil. The Book fell open to me.

The rabble-rousers hated me. I had the longest horns in the country because I was using the very book they were using. I turned the guns the other way, as it were. I interpreted as I thought the prophets would interpret it, given the situation.

"We have a religious phenomenon in America that has its origin in the South. Established churches followed urban trends. People out here were isolated and delivered religion on the basis of what they saw. Store-bought clothes—which they could not buy out of poverty—became worldly and sinful: 'We had rather be beggars in the House of the Lord than dwell in king's palaces.' They were denied schooling. They were called rednecks and crackers and damn niggers. But the Bible was God's Book. Refused access to medical aid, faith healed the body as well as the soul: 'We seek another world.' It was a protest against things economically unavailable. I interpreted this protest and related it to the Bible—instead of calling them hillbillies and rednecks.

"At one gathering five or six Klansmen were around. I said, 'I want to speak about the Ku Klux Klan.' All the people who are in the Klan are not vicious. My brother was a member. You try to reach people at the consciousness of their needs. I quoted Peter on the day of Pentecost: 'Save yourselves, don't wait for somebody else.' Peter made contact with every person in the language in which he was born. I won over a number of Klansmen.

"I translated the democratic impulse of mass religion rather than its protofascist content into a language they understood. That's what got me in trouble with the synod. I was on trial. They asked me how I felt about the divinity of Jesus. I said, 'I believe in the divinity but not the deity of Jesus.' They didn't know the difference. The divinity is God's likeness, the deity is Godship. I had the Son of Man as a carpenter.

"The preachers tell a story from the Bible, entertain for an hour or so and then come back to it. Young radicals try to clarify every issue in one speech. People are confused, go out and scratch their heads. And the kid says: What's the matter with those dumb people? The demagogues are smarter—they entertain. I've tried to beat them at their own game. But you've got to know where to check the emotion."

In Winston-Salem, when we went out to organize the tobacco workers, the leader said: "If you crack this in two years, it'll be a miracle." We went to the oldest church. It was a bitter night. The pastor was a white woman sitting there with an army blanket around her shoulders and a little old hat. I knew she was the bellwether. Unless I got her, I got nobody.

I gave the gospel of the Kings: Good News is only good when it feeds the poor. This woman pastor got up and drawled: "Well, this is the first time I heard the gospel of three square meals a day, and I want in on it. I love to shout and now I know every time I shout, I know I need shoes." First thing I know, she was touching cadence and going way off.

I jumped up and said, "Wait." (He unwinds into a rapid-fire sermon.) "I charge you before the Lord and Saviour, Jesus Christ, who will judge the quick and the dead. Preach the Word. Thy word is truth, truth is thy word. Being instant, inside season, out of season, reprove, rebuke, for the time will come, Sister Price, the time will come for the kings. When they heap to themselves teachers, and theologians endowed by robber barons, to take people from the people, boys and girls, and teach them to take orders, and not to discuss controversial subjects as to offend—and to say: 'Don't believe there's such a thing as poverty. Boss John has your best interests at heart. And if you die of fatigue or malnutrition or pneumonia or lack of medical care, your most precious soul will be borne on the wings of lily-white angels in a home 140 million light years away.' Turn away from truth and we'll be turned away. Sister Price, we can't turn away from truth. We'll sing a song." (He sings.) "Let the will of the Lord be done—in the home, in the school, in the church, in the union. . . ."

I had to translate this emotion into action. But if I'd let her go on shouting, we'd never have made it. In three months, they called a labor board election. We won. We called on the Bible and the Son of Man.

VII. DEATH

In many ways, the Depression was hardest of all on the old. It often destroyed the savings and plans of a lifetime, unsettled long-familiar habits and routines, severed old associations, and challenged dearly and deeply held beliefs. The following selection presents a short biography of elderly people whose lives were badly disrupted by the Depression. In what ways did it change their lives? What were the hardest things to bear? How much help did they receive from their families? From their former employers? From the government? What was their attitude toward relief? Does it differ from the attitudes of the unemployed workers whose case histories appear elsewhere in this collection?

From Jessie A. Bloodworth and Elizabeth J. Greenwood, The Personal Side *(mimeograph, Works Progress Administration, 1939), 90-105.*

INTERVIEWING COMPLETED
DECEMBER 13, 1937

Mr. Beuscher, 62 years old, had been working for 29 years for the Dubuque railroad shops when they closed in 1931. He was recalled to work at the shops after he had been unemployed for 4 years. Tall, gangling, weather-beaten, he stoops forward when he talks so that he may follow the conversation with greater ease, for he is more than a little deaf. He expresses opinions decisively and vigorously, his black eyes gleaming from under bushy black brows.

BEUSCHER

At home

Mr. Beuscher	62
Mrs. Beuscher	60
Paul	13
Katherine	17
Jeannette	19
Bob	21

Married and away from home

Charles	23
Celia	25
Butch	26
Eileen	28
Helen	30
Caroline	32

Mrs. Beuscher is 2 years younger than her husband. She is the mother of 11 children, but has found time to make dresses and coats and suits, not only for her own family, but also for customers outside the home. A genial, mild-mannered woman, she is earnest in her speech, but always ready to laugh at her own and other people's foibles. Her eyes, merry but tired, are protected with spectacles that slide down on the bridge of her nose when she bends over reading or sewing and that are pushed up on her forehead when she raises her head to talk or to listen to an especially amusing radio program.

Four children remain at home: Bob, 21, a high school graduate, has had only short-time employment and is now out of work; Jeannette, who completed a high school commercial course last spring, is now clerking in a 5-and-10-cent store on Saturdays; Katherine, a high school junior who goes out occasionally with her "boy friend," cleans the house on Saturday mornings; Paul, attending junior high

school, is privileged as one of the "Knothole Gang" to see the local
ball games at 10¢ a game and contributes his proceeds from the sale
of magazines, sometimes as much as "a whole 15¢," to his mother's
purse.

One daughter died several years ago. The other children are married and now have their own households. But during the early years
of the depression Charles, then unmarried, was at home; and Celia
and Butch, who had had their own homes, came with their families to
the Beuscher home when they could no longer pay rent.

Mr. Beuscher was educated haphazardly in country schools in
Wisconsin during the seasons when work was not too pressing on his
father's farm and his "old man" didn't "make him saw wood" in preference to sending him to school. He worked as a "hand" on his
father's and neighboring farms until he came to Dubuque, with his
wife and two children, in 1902. He was employed at the boat works
for a few weeks before being taken on as a boilermaker's helper in
the railroad shops. Promoted to a job as boilermaker in 1910, he
continued at the same job, except for brief interruptions because of
illness, a disagreement with his foreman, and, again, a general
railroad strike, until the closing of the shops in 1931.

When Mr. Beuscher began work in the shops as a boilermaker's
helper in 1902, he was paid 10-1/2¢ an hour for a 60-hour week,
though he actually worked but 55 hours, for Saturday afternoons
were free. In those days jobs in the railroad shops were more plen-
tiful than job-seekers, for there was much work to be done and the
pay was so low that the shops could not successfully compete for
workers with neighboring factories.

Such a thing as a standard wage was unknown, for this was before
the time of shop unions, and the highest paid of all the boilermakers
in the shop earned only 29¢ an hour. There had been "floaters"
before 1905, but it was not until that year that workers in the Dubuque shops were organized. In the beginning all of the helpers were
organized in a separate union; only later were the boilermakers' helpers taken into the boilermakers' union, blacksmiths' helpers into the
blacksmiths' union, and so on. When the helpers were first banded
together, Mr. Beuscher, representing the boilermakers' helpers, along
with two representatives of the other helpers, went to Chicago to
negotiate for wage increases. They were successful in a measure, for

irregular increases were granted; a standard wage came only much later.

The effect of organization on Mr. Beuscher's own wage rate was to increase it to 18¢ an hour. Mr. Beuscher attributes the general wage increases for shop workers in 1908 partly to the rising cost of living which had its effect on wages in various industries and partly to increasing union strength. He is a staunch believer in craft unionism and in the A. F. L.; he would not belong to the boilermakers' union if it were affiliated with the CIO, which to him symbolizes "one big union" and the interference of men skilled in one craft with the actual methods of work of those skilled in other crafts. There is disagreement, good-tempered but vigorous, between Mr. Beuscher and his 21-year-old son on this score; Bob believes that the CIO may help to equalize wages by reducing differentials in rates.

Mr. Beucher's highest earnings as boilermaker's helper amounted to 28-1/2¢ an hour. In 1910 he became a boilermaker, earning 40-1/2¢ an hour for a 10-hour day. It was in 1913 that hours were shortened to 9 a day. During the World War Mr. Beuscher's wage rate was increased several times, finally reaching a peak of 72¢ an hour. The ground gained during the war was held but only with a struggle; rates were reduced 5¢ an hour for a short period after the war, but pay-cuts were soon restored. In 1922 an announced pay reduction led to a general railroad strike, the only one affecting the Dubuque shops since the "Debs strike of '94." The strike was short-lived and successful, so far as the workers' effort to avoid a general wage reduction was concerned; Mr. Beuscher continued to earn 72¢ an hour until the shops closed in 1931 and earnings ceased altogether.

During the 29 years that Mr. Beuscher was regularly employed in the shops, the family managed to live comfortably and happily, though they never had "luxuries"—they "never had a car"—and never got very far ahead, for with 11 growing children, frequent unanticipated bills, such as doctors' bills and dentists' bills, had to be met. But Mrs. Beuscher enjoyed planning in advance for small purchases from the "next pay"—curtains for the living room windows or special items of clothing—even though the plans could not always be carried through. Almost every weekend the Beuschers had guests or visited their friends; "the children didn't stop us from going."

In 1915 the Beuschers bought an attractive though unpretentious seven-room frame cottage on a payment-purchase plan. Until Mr. Beuscher lost his job, he paid $20 monthly to the real estate agency carrying the mortgage; this amount covered payments on the principal and interest of 7 percent. The home is in a north end neighborhood of well-kept single-family houses occupied for the most part by industrial wage-earners with families. Piece by piece the Beuschers' home has been comfortably furnished, and it gives evidence of the care and planning that have gone into its making.

The Beuschers never had a savings account—they thought it more practical to pay as much as possible on the house, especially as the rate of interest on the mortgage exceeded that on savings accounts—but they did invest in insurance policies for all members of the family. As the 10-payment life insurance policies carried for the older children had matured, they had been cashed in, but premiums on policies carried for Mr. and Mrs. Beuscher and the four youngest children were kept paid up to date until the spring of 1931, when the Beuschers found themselves with a mortgaged home, five children still largely dependent on the parents, and no regular income.

As they "look back on it," Mr. and Mrs. Beuscher scarcely know how they did manage to get along during the time that he had no regular work. The irregular income from Mrs. Beuscher's sewing continued, though she was forced to lower prices until earnings averaged no more than $3 or $4 a week. Instead of buying any new clothing, Mrs. Beuscher made over the old dresses and coats which, though discarded, had been packed away in the attic trunks. Insurance policies were cashed in one by one. Mrs. Beuscher's 20-payment life insurance policy, with face value of $500, netted her $137; cash surrender values of the four policies carried on the younger children averaged about $35. Though they were able to keep Mr. Beuscher's policy, $200 was borrowed against the face value of $1,000. Premiums have now been paid to date, but interest on the loan has been deducted from the value, now no more than $600.

For a year after Mr. Beuscher lost his job, the family's only cash income was the four hundred seventy-odd dollars obtained from the insurance policies and Mrs. Beuscher's irregular earnings, as contrasted with the pre-depression regular income of about $130 a month, Mr. Beuscher's full-time earnings. In spite of all the Beuschers could do to reduce expenses and to raise cash, not all of the bills could be met: payments due on the principal of the mortgage and the property taxes had to be disregarded, and Mr. and Mrs. Beuscher were harassed with worry over the $68 grocery bill, for they had never before asked for credit, except from week to week. Expenditures for replacements of household equipment were eliminated from the budget. By the time Mr. Beuscher returned to work, the family had almost no bedding; this was the first special item purchased when the family again had a regular income from private employment.

Although they had heard about other families, some of them in their own neighborhood, who had applied for relief grants, the Beuschers had never thought of requesting relief for themselves until one day, in the fall of 1933, Mr. Beuscher came home from a neighbor's to say to his wife, "Do you know what Jim said? He said we ought to try to get relief." Mrs. Beuscher was so "shocked" that she gasps, even 4 years later, when she recalls her emotion. But after talking things over, Mr. and Mrs. Beuscher agreed that application for relief was a virtual necessity. Mr. Beuscher remembers going down to the courthouse for the first time as the hardest thing he ever had to do in his life; his hand was "on the door-knob five times" before he turned it. The investigation, which the Beuschers recognized as necessary and inevitable, was so prolonged that Mrs. Beuscher "really didn't think" that the family would ever get relief. But finally, after about 2 months, a grocery order of $4.50 was granted. Mrs. Beuscher had long before learned to "manage" excellently on little, and though the order was meager, the family "got along" and "always had enough to eat." Mrs. Beuscher believes that investigators "did the best they could"; she resents only their insistence on the disconnection of the telephone, on which she depended for keeping in touch with her customers.

Soon Mr. Beuscher was assigned as a laborer to county relief work, for which he was paid, always in grocery orders, $7.20 a week; this increased amount gave the family a little more leeway. Yet they were still without much cash. Payments even of interest on the mortgage had had to cease. Because they anticipated foreclosure of the mortgage, the Beuschers applied for a Home Owners loan, which was refused, since there seemed to be little chance of Mr. Beuscher's getting back to work. "Things looked pretty bad then," and Mr.

Beuscher was considered a "bad risk" because of his age. Though Mr. and Mrs. Beuscher were "terribly disappointed at the time," they are glad now that they are not burdened with such a debt.

Mrs. Beuscher cannot guess how the family could have managed during the depression without the home, but Mr. Beuscher found home ownership more of a handicap than a help, for relief grants made no allowance for taxes or interest payments, while "bums" who had never tried to save or look to the future had their rent paid "regularly."

While the relief grants continued, a married daughter whose husband, as a collection agent, found his commissions going lower and lower, and a married son, who "hadn't a sign of a job," moved in with the parents. There were then 13 living in the 7 room house. Of course, the children had come home only after a general discussion in which it was agreed that this was the best plan, and everyone had thought of the arrangement as quite "temporary"; actually Celia and Butch and their families remained in the household for about a year. For a time, Eliot, the son-in-law, was able to contribute $5 a week, which probably covered any additional expenditures for himself and his wife and their two children, although there was no attempt to keep separate household accounts. But soon he could make no collections at all, and payments to the Beuschers ceased.

Eliot and Butch found that they could not obtain relief grants for their families while they remained with the Beuschers, nor could the grant for the entire household be increased. They did all they could to help the family: worked with Mr. Beuscher for the gas company to pay the gas bills, and for the coal company to pay the coal bills; they worked in the garden and helped to saw wood for the family's use.

For a time Charles was able to contribute a little to the family income by playing ball on professional teams in various towns; almost every week end during the baseball season he accumulated $7 or $8 in this way. But since he could find no regular work in Dubuque, he soon went to Detroit, where he stayed with a married sister. Though it was not absolutely necessary for him to leave home, in his absence there was "one less mouth to feed," and he was in a better position to seek work. He has since paid his back board bills to his sister, and is now married and working in a neighboring Iowa town.

The family's garden, for which the city furnished some of the seeds and the plot of ground on the city island, added fresh vegetables to the list of staples which alone could be purchased on the grocery orders; there were even some vegetables to be sold from house to house, and Mrs. Beuscher canned a little almost every day, just as the vegetables were ready for use. One summer she put up 500 quarts of vegetables. The family had never had a garden before 1932, both because there was little space and because they had "never thought of it," but Mr. Beuscher has continued to garden even now that he is back at work. Since the island garden plot could be reached only by boat, transportation was something of a problem, solved when Mr. Beuscher and three of his neighbors chipped in $2 apiece for the materials from which they built a jointly-owned boat. Only infrequently did two or more families set out to work in their gardens at the same time; so they were forever having to halloo across the water to ask that the boat be brought back to the town side to pick up more gardeners.

Grocery orders were supplemented with surplus commodities. The only other outside assistance which the family received was a sack of seed potatoes for Mr. Beuscher's garden planting in the spring of 1932 and several tons of coal during the winter of 1933-34 from a private charitable organization to which the Beuschers had in previous years contributed with the thought that they were "giving something away"; now they consider these contributions the "best investment they ever made"; they have been "repaid a hundred-fold."

Although the Beuschers never felt comfortable about receiving relief, it came to be more or less an accepted thing. "You know, you went down to City Hall, and had to wait in line, and you saw all your friends; it was funny in a way, though it was pitiful, too. . . . People went down to the relief office, and talked about going, just the way they might have gone anywhere else."

The family received food orders for only a few months, as Mr. Beuscher was soon assigned to the CWA Eagle Point Park project as a laborer, earning 40¢ an hour. Later he worked on the lock and dam project at 50¢ an hour. Mr. Beuscher cannot understand why there was so great a difference between the wage rates of laborers on work projects and those of skilled carpenters. Although he was glad to be assigned to projects, there was little essential difference in his feelings about direct relief and about "work relief"; he worked hard for his pay, but still felt that he was being "given something." He has heard many times that persons on relief do not want work and will not accept jobs in private industry, but he knows from project employees whose reactions were similar to his that such is not the case, except perhaps in a very few instances. Nothing makes him "more mad" than this criticism of project workers.

Mrs. Beuscher believes that relief, as such, has not fostered dependency. "Of course, there have always been some people who have wanted something for nothing," but "the right kind of people—the people we know, except maybe a very few—" have invariably tried to remain independent, applied for relief only as a last resort, and made every effort to go back to private employment. It may be true that some persons have become so discouraged and disheartened that they have ceased to look for jobs, but any such discouragement Mrs. Beuscher considers "purely temporary." Men will go back to private employment as soon as there are jobs to be had "without standing in line day after day waiting" on the chance that someone may be hired from among the men at the factory gates.

On principle, Mr. Beuscher decidedly favors work projects as against direct relief. "Men should be made to work for what they get," and the "majority of them—at least 70 percent—" prefer to work. In any event, however, Mr. Beuscher believes that some direct relief will always be necessary as there are a "few people who aren't eligible for pensions and can't work."

Some time before the time that Mr. Beuscher was called back to work at the railroad shops, Eliot and Butch had reestablished a household for their two families. They received relief for a time, but finally both found work in local factories, and Butch moved to a home of his own. Now, they are independent, as are the Beuschers, senior.

Bob tried at various times to be assigned to a CCC camp. The family does not fully understand the many delays, though they believe that boys from smaller family groups were sent in preference to Bob because other families were more demanding and insistent than the Beuschers. But Bob's turn finally came in the fall of 1935. He liked the woods work, except when the temperature was well below zero. During a prolonged cold spell he asked for and was granted a transfer to kitchen duty. He was chagrined when the temperature dropped still lower, and the woods workers were permitted to loaf indoors while he labored in the kitchen where the thermometer stood at 5 above zero. Again he requested a transfer, which was arranged just as the weather warmed up enough for the woods workers to be sent out every day. On the whole, he considers it quite a joke that he managed always to choose "the wrong thing." He was enjoying the work most "just when he came home," after a 10-month stay, to take a job as a saw-operator, paying 30¢ an hour, with the Mississippi Milling Company. Several increases had brought his hourly rate up to 37¢ when he was laid off because of a general reduction in the force in August 1936. During the winter months the plant "took on every kid they could find"; then when the warehouse was overstocked the younger workers were laid off in great numbers.

Although Mr. and Mrs. Beuscher "don't say the depression is over yet," times have been better for them since the late fall of 1935, when Mr. Beuscher was called back to his old work at the shops at the old rate of pay. Mr. Beuscher considers this "regular work," and, as such, far superior to relief work, especially as he now "feels more independent." Still, it is not as it was in the old days when 1,500 men were employed rebuilding damaged and out-worn cars. Of the 130 men taken back at the shop, only 25 remain at work, which now consists of wrecking instead of reclamation, and no one of the 25 men knows how long his work will last. Mr. Beuscher was one of those to be recalled and to remain at work because of his "seniority right."

While he was out of work, Mr. Beuscher had regularly made the rounds of the local factories looking for jobs and had kept active his registration with the State employment office. Though he frequently grew discouraged with looking for work, Mrs. Beuscher thinks that he "enjoyed it in a way." He and his neighbors used to get together in the evenings, air their many disappointments, and decide not to bother going out again to look for jobs. But invariably the following morning found them "off again." When Mr. Beuscher learned that a few men were to be rehired, he went to the shops to explain that he was available. Soon, he was called back. Since his return to work, the Beuschers have paid up all back bills, including interest on the mortgage, property taxes, and street assessments which totaled about $500. Within the past month, the Beuschers have been able to claim the deed to their home, as the principal of the mortgage has been reduced to $1,500. The interest rate from now on will be only 5-1/2 instead of 7 percent.

Mrs. Beuscher thinks that perhaps young people have had the most discouraging experiences in the search for work. After Bob was laid off at the mill, he made every effort to find other employment. He reported regularly at the State employment office, which referred him to only one job, a job as chronometer reader for a battery factory. Bob thought that he could do the work, as he had had some practice in chronometer reading in his high school machine shop work, but when he reported at the factory he was told that only a man of 35 years and 200 pounds could be employed. "The local factories will not file applications" and usually offer jobs only to those men who are waiting at the plants when openings occur. Thus, when the word goes around that some factory is "hiring"—which may mean only that one man, perhaps "a relative" of another employee, has been taken on the day before—the men all go to the factory to wait for jobs. Bob has spent many hours and days "waiting" at the gates of factories in Dubuque and in Illinois towns to which he has either hitchhiked or traveled on the family's railroad pass.

Bob has thought of going to Detroit, where he would live with one of his sisters while hunting work, but Mrs. Beuscher tells him, "If you don't have a job, your place is at home, not with your brothers-in-law, who have a hard enough time taking care of their own families." One of the brothers-in-law has recently had his hours at the factory cut in half.

Finally, Bob heard that an insulating company was expanding and taking on more men. Next morning he went to the plant at 7 o'clock; he stayed all day. Of the 30 men waiting, only 1 was hired. On the second day Bob was given a job weighing and carting raw materials. He had worked 1 full 8-hour day and about 2 hours of the second working day when some of the machinery broke down and the plant was closed for repairs.

Jeannette, like Bob, has kept a registration active at the State employment office. She is now clerking on Saturdays in a 5-and-10 cent store and hopes to have several days' work just before Christmas. Although she would prefer stenographic work, she says that she has been willing to take what she can get. She talks to the other kids and knows that none of her friends has a regular full-time clerical job.

Mrs. Beuscher believes that "the depression has changed people's outlook." In a way she is more "comfortable" now than when both she and Mr. Beuscher worried about bills and tried to plan for the future. Now, they "just live from day to day," with the feeling that since they "lived through the depression" they can face anything to come. Of course, it was fun to plan and look ahead, "and that's one way we've lost." This resignation and acceptance of what the future may bring, Mrs. Beuscher accounts a "sign of age" as well as a result of the depression. Another "sign of age" is Mr. and Mrs. Beuscher's being content to spend leisure time at home; lack of money "was the start of it," and when they were once again reasonably secure, they had "lost the ambition to go."

Mr. and Mrs. Beuscher would prefer to live through another and longer depression rather than a war, which they fear may be inevitable. All wars he considers only "legalized stealing," the result of "capital" and "greed." "If the U.S. were actually invaded," Mr. Beuscher says, I "would take up a gun myself." He sees no reason, however, for anyone's fighting "across the sea."

Mr. Beuscher is intensely interested in discussions of the causes of extensive unemployment. As a reader of 5¢ weeklies he cannot agree with "editorial writers" that there is no serious "technological unemployment." From his own experience, Mr. Beuscher knows the work of many men has been taken over by machinery. When he first worked as a helper, it was a good 10-hour job for 3 men to hammer by hand 300 rivets; after the introduction of pneumatic drills, 1,200 rivets could be placed in the same length of time with about the same effort. Once a freight train crew of 5 men handled about 20 cars; now a crew may be responsible for 5 times as many cars, "and not the old 40-ton cars, either, but 60-, 80- or 100-ton cars." And so it goes, in railroad shops, on the trains, and in other industries as well. Though it has been claimed that displaced workers are absorbed by new industries, Mr. Beuscher believes that the proper balance has not been maintained, as the new machinery wears longer than the old and need not be produced is such great quantity.

Mr. Beuscher has only one suggested solution for the problem of unemployment: persons of "wealth" should be persuaded to invest their money in industries that might increase or create new employment. He believes also that there should be a better "distribution" of the money paid for commodities. But Mr. Beuscher does not hold "radical" ideas. At one time there was quite a group of Socialists in

Dubuque; now the movement has "died out." Mr. Beuscher expresses his feeling about the group by telling gleefully an old story. A friend of Mr. Beuscher's approached one of these Socialists, who had a remarkably fine garden, and asked, "John, you believe in distribution, don't you?" "Yes." "Then I want you to give me your carrots and cabbages."

Mr. and Mrs. Beuscher are agreed that they would not in any event be willing to give up property which they might have struggled to accumulate. However, they would not want great wealth, as they would scarcely know how to spend or handle it. Mr. Beuscher is nearing his 63d birthday; at 65 he will be eligible for a Railroad Retirement pension of $62 or $63 a month, the precise amount depending on the extent of his earnings during the intervening period. His greatest present hope is that he can work steadily until he reaches the age of 65; his greatest fear, that the work will peter out between one day and the next. When he leaves the shop, Mr. Beuscher would like to be able to buy a small plot of ground, but this is only a wish, not an expectation. He would not want to go back to farming as a renter or laborer, but he would like to farm if he could own his land, just enough to work comfortably with his efforts alone.

Though the Beuschers are reasonably well satisfied with remaining in Dubuque, they consider it "the cheapest town there is," so far as wages go. The local factories have "never paid what they should, but then rents are low here, too." Mr. Beuscher thinks that he would not be "telling anything" by explaining the reason for the low wage scale, for "everybody knows that a few factories control the town." Mrs. Beuscher says with some dismay that she has read recently that "even office workers in Dubuque get less than in any other city in the United States." Then she rises to the defense of the town, which has "good schools" and a comparatively new radio station; it numbers among its famous people a movie star, the wife of a movie star, and a great football player. On the whole, "it's not a bad place to live"; and anyhow, the family "can't leave now because you even have to pay to get across the toll bridges" into the adjacent States of Wisconsin and Illinois.

Employment Chronology for Mr. Beuscher

Until 1902	On father's farm.
1902-1931	Helper and boilermaker, railroad shops.
Spring 1931 fall 1935	Unemployed except for emergency work.
Fall 1935 present	Boilermaker, railroad shops.

Social workers were a new element in many families' lives in the 1930s, but the new is usually most troubling to the elderly. The following selection suggests some of the difficulties that old people had with new government assistance programs, and vice versa. What does the government's role with regard to the elderly suggest about the family structure of modern America? Why was there such a "dread of an institution," and a "dread of a pauper's burial" among the old? What values did old people struggle most to maintain in the face of hardship?

From Gertrude Springer, "Too Old to Change," The Survey *71 (June 1935), 173-4.*

"Well, if that's you social workers' idea of old-age assistance, to leave a sick old woman and three dogs alone in a wreck of a house just because she doesn't want to move out. . . ."

Miss Bailey gulped. She had so gratefully accepted the "loan" of herself to the new old-age assistance board as a vacation from the pressures of the home-relief division—yet here on her doorstep was the same old human equation, complete with irate citizen. She could understand his irritation. The old house, its windows broken, its roof sagging, its yard a tangle of weeds, was truly a neighborhood eyesore; the mongrel dogs were a nuisance, and it did seem inhuman to leave old Miss Seldon—"old witch" the jeering children called her—alone there now that her legs had given out and she could no longer totter around and take care of herself.

"What would you have us do, Mr. Thompson? Carry her out by main force kicking and screaming? That seems pretty rough treatment for a woman of eighty."

Mr. Thompson dodged that one, but was sure that somebody ought to make the old woman see reason—or something.

"And you think we haven't tried?" Miss Bailey turned the pages of the case record. "The neighbors have tried, and the doctor, and the minister; the visiting nurse tries every time she goes there and so does the social worker. We've all tried for three months, ever since she took to her bed. But old Miss Seldon has lived in that house for fifty years; her parents died there. It is the 'roof over my head' that so many old people think makes them safe. She's forgotten that the mortgage was foreclosed three years ago and that the bank has let her stay on because it isn't worth while to make her move."

"But the old woman is helpless. The neighbors have to look out for her. She might die alone." Mr. Thompson was far from persuaded.

"She might, and probably much more peacefully than if she were dragged off to a hospital. Indeed all she asks is to be let die in her own home."

"Her own home!" from a less dignified person than Mr. Thompson this would have been a snort.

"Absolutely," Miss Bailey had found what she was looking for in the record—a letter feebly penciled on blue-lined paper. "For she doesn't see that house as we see it, or herself either. About six weeks ago, we told her that it was possible that her $30 a month old-age allowance would not be continued unless she agreed to hospital care. It was then she wrote to Mrs. Roosevelt."

"To Mrs. Roosevelt!"

"Why yes—they all do, hundreds of the old, the poor, the infirm write her their troubles with the most complete faith in her understanding and her ability to do something for them. We get these letters constantly, forwarded from the White House. And very often they show us states of mind that our workers in their hurried visits could not possibly know. Now here's old Miss Seldon's letter. She tells about her 'ancestral home'—she doesn't realize it's tumbling down and is no longer hers—about her dogs, 'all I have left to love,' about her garden, 'with the roses my mother planted,' and about the neighborhood children—she doesn't know they jeer, she says 'The children would miss me.' And must her home, which is all she has to live for, be broken up, she asks, because she is having a little spell of her old trouble with her legs?''

"And I suppose Mrs. Roosevelt told you to let her stay?''

"Oh, no. It was Miss Seldon herself by this letter who made us realize how unimportant physical discomforts are to her compared to the emotional satisfaction of being in her own home. She's happy lying there alone. Surely at eighty she might be allowed to make the choice.''

"But the house is an eyesore to the whole neighborhood!''

"Yes, I know, and the community has its rights. But that house has been an eyesore for a good many years. Surely the neighbors can be patient just a little longer. She's eighty. It doesn't seem worth while to try to change her, does it?''

As old-age relief takes root as a permanent form of public assistance social workers in increasing numbers are being drawn into its administration, and are finding in it new challenges to their experience, their technique and their understanding. The great majority of the cases offer of course no complications. The monthly check, its very regularity carrying a sense of security, enables the old person to hold his life together in his own way. The principal function of the social worker then is to see to it that he is not exploited and does not suffer for lack of medical care. But just when the work begins to seem relatively simple along comes a case that requires such insight into human motivation, such facility of interpretation and such imaginative use of community resources that the best case-work skills are none too good. This is particularly true, say experienced workers, in small communities where the tax-payer thinks the old-age pension should be an instrument for reform.

"I sometimes think that our hardest and most important job is in-

terpreting old people to the community and vice versa'' said a worker
in an up-state New York county. ''The minute an old-age allowance
comes in the door of some tarpaper shack the community becomes
very concerned about the life that goes on there though it has probably gone on for years without anyone bothering about it. We have
a case, old Pete Johnson and his wife, that the town is determined
shall be moved out of their terrible tin-can cabin on the river bank.
But the Johnsons are perfectly contented where they are, their sole
fear being that they will lose the only home they've known for years.
You wouldn't believe how much time and tact it has taken to induce
them to placate the community by cleaning up a little and by planting
morning-glories to run over the house and, on the other hand, the effort it has been to persuade the townspeople to leave them where
they are for the summer. We'll cross next winter's bridge when we get
to it. There is no real community interest at stake—the danger of fire
or infection for instance—so we are trying to go slowly.''

The greatest anxiety of the people on the old-age relief rolls,
greater even than their dread of an institution, is their dread of
pauper burial. In fact much of the dread of an institution seems to
spring from the fear that it leads directly to the potter's field.

''The hardships and deprivations that old people undergo to hang
onto money for a decent burial are beyond belief,'' said a worker in
an eastern state. ''Some of our old people have no funds of their own
and the county must bury them, but most of them have accumulated
their burial money in a savings bank or in the form of insurance. The
state has a legal claim against this fund, usually small, but it does not
press it while the old person lives. After his death the funeral costs
are a first charge on it. In this state a maximum of $125 is allowed; it
is more in some states, less in others. Whatever is left reverts to the
state as reimbursement for the funds expended for maintenance. But
what a time we have making an old person understand that he can
trust the good faith of the state in this transaction and that in taking
from the state the means to go on living he is not sacrificing the—to
him—more precious assurance of dignified burial. Young workers
are, we find, apt to be impatient with this concern of the aged but
unless they can accept it they'll find they have a lot to learn in this
work.

''Our allowances are of course budgeted to need, taking into account any contributions from relatives and so on, but sometimes an old person seems to think he needs a funeral more than the things we think he needs. We have a case now that is a puzzler—an old woman without kith or kin who came to us from a little church society, her only possession a burial insurance of $125, exactly what this state allows in exemption of assets for funeral expenses. But it seemed that this was only half enough for the ritualistic funeral old Mrs. Tobey had set her heart on. And do you know what that old woman did? By unbelievable deprivations she began saving out of her allowance, at best just enough to keep her going, to get that $250 funeral. We knew something was wrong—it was obvious that she was slowly starving—but we couldn't put a finger on the trouble.

"Then, when she had her additional $125 in hand, the story came out. And was she proud and happy! But here is the point. Under our rules anything she possesses above the $125 burial allowance will at her death revert to the state. The old woman believes that that extra $125 is her own money as much as her burial policy because she all but starved to get it. But the law doesn't see it that way, and no one living could make her understand. To tell you the truth we haven't tried. And she is beginning to fatten up."

The hope that old-age pensions would empty the alms houses and shelters of their old folk has not been realized. In Massachusetts the population of the town infirmaries is increasing and new ones are being built, the reason being, say the authorities, that while the allowances keep many people out of institutions they also uncover many cases of a kind which require institutional care and treatment. In Pennsylvania, as in other states, the effort to get old men out of the shelters and onto allowances has been balked by such detailed provisions of the law as that a man must not have deserted his wife within fifteen years or been a "professional" tramp or beggar within two years. A quick study of 4000 men of all ages in a city shelter when the Pennsylvania law went into effect indicated that not more than 150 would be found eligible for allowances. Yet to every old person in an institution the news that a law has been passed holds out infinite hope that regardless of his infirmities he can again live his own life.

"About as trying a task as we have," said a worker in a state where old-age relief is just getting into its stride, "is to make some worn-out old fellow see that he is better off in the City Home than he could possibly be outside on an old-age allowance. Just last week we had to turn down a man—and I still wish we had worked out a budget for him and let him try. He was so certain he could get by if he had even $5 a week. Many's the week before he came to the Home, he said, when he hadn't had as much. But he didn't realize that in five years senility had crept up on him, and that his spells of "blind staggers' came oftener than they used to. It certainly wouldn't have been sensible to let him leave the home and yet I wish we had. He could always have come back.

"As a matter of fact many of the old men who leave the Home and try to manage on an allowance do come back, especially if they have been there a good while. They find life outside confused and lonely; they come back for companionship, for someone to talk to.

"When there seems a reasonable prospect of an old man making the grade on his own we give him a chance to reopen his old contacts and to see what arrangements he can make before the institutional bridge is burned. We make it as easy as we can for him to go and easier still for him to come back. But all our experience indicates that it is the very exceptional person past seventy, in an institution for several years, who can pick up his life again outside on the terms that his infirmities impose."

As experience accumulates in the administration of old-age assistance, relatively new in America, workers are becoming convinced that the fewer controls thrown around the old people the better. The "government pension" as the old folk invariably call it, brings to most of them the chance to build a little nest of security where they live out their lives in their own way. "It may sometimes seem to us a pretty poor nest," say the workers, "and we may itch to show them how to make it wider and brighter and better. But if they are satisfied it is stupid for us to try to impose our ideas. It would serve no real social purpose. The most we can do is to guard the peace and security that 'government pensions' have brought them."

VIII. EPILOGUE: LOOKING BACKWARD

The Depression left an indelible mark on those who lived through it—an "invisible scar," as one historian has put it. The final two selections are the reminiscences of a man and a woman, respectively, whose lives ever since have been colored by the crisis of the 1930s. How did it change their outlook on life? What are its most lasting effects? How has the memory of the Depression influenced their judgment about the present?

Both selections are from Studs Terkel, Hard Times: An Oral History of the Great Depression (*New York: Pantheon,* 1970), 412-23, 461-62.

WARD JAMES

He is seventy-three. He teaches at a fashionable private school for boys, out East. He was born in Wisconsin: attended school there.

BEFORE THE CRASH, I was with a small publishing house in New York. I was in charge of all the production and did most of the copy. It was a good job. The company was growing. It looked like a permanent situation. I was feeling rather secure.

I realized that people weren't secure in the publishing business. There was no tenure. We didn't have any union. That was the first move I made, organizing the Book and Magazine Union in New York. A lot of white collar people at the time felt unions were not for them. They were above it.

Until 1935, I had my job with this publishing house. They insisted

I take a month vacation without pay and a few other things, but it wasn't really too distressing. It became tougher and tougher.

I was fired. No reasons given. I think my work with the union had a good deal to do with it, although I couldn't prove it. What hurt was that I'd gotten pretty good in writing technical books for boys. I had three published. By now, with things getting tight, no publisher wanted any book that wouldn't be a best seller.

I was out of work for six months. I was losing my contacts as well as my energy. I kept going from one publishing house to another. I never got past the telephone operator. It was just wasted time. One of the worst things was occupying your time, sensibly. You'd go to the library. You took a magazine to the room and sat and read. I didn't have a radio. I tried to do some writing and found I couldn't concentrate. The day was long. There was nothing to do evenings. I was going around in circles, it was terrifying. So I just vegetated.

With some people I knew, there was a coldness, shunning: I'd rather not see you just now. Maybe *I'll* lose my job next week. On the other hand, I made some very close friends, who were merely acquaintances before. If I needed $5 for room rent or something, it was available.

I had a very good friend who cashed in his bonus bonds to pay his rent. I had no bed, so he let me sleep there. (Laughs.) I remember getting down to my last pair of pants, which looked awful. One of my other friends had just got a job and had an extra pair of pants that fit me, so I inherited them. (Laughs.)

I went to apply for unemployment insurance, which had just been put into effect. I went three weeks in succession. It still hadn't come through. Then I discovered the catch. At that time, anybody who earned more than $3,000 a year was not paid unemployment insurance unless his employer had O.K.'d it. It could be withheld. My employer exercised his option of not O.K.'ing it. He exercised his vindictive privilege. I don't think that's the law any more.

I finally went on relief. It's an experience I don't want anybody to go through. It comes as close to crucifixion as. . . . You sit in an auditorium and are given a number. The interview was utterly ridiculous and mortifying. In the middle of mine, a more dramatic guy than I dived from the second floor stairway, head first, to demonstrate he was gonna get on relief even if he had to go to the hospital to do it.

There were questions like: Who are your friends? Where have you been living? Where's your family? I had sent my wife and child to her folks in Ohio, where they could live more simply. Why should anybody give you money? Why should anybody give you a place to sleep? What sort of friends? This went on for half an hour. I got angry and said, "Do you happen to know what a friend is?" He changed his attitude very shortly. I did get certified sometime later. I think they paid $9 a month.

I came away feeling I didn't have any business living any more. I was imposing on somebody, a great society or something like that.

That ended with a telegram from Chicago, from the Illinois Writers Project. I had edited a book for the director, who knew my work. He needed a top editor to do final editorial work on the books being published, particularly the Illinois Guide. I felt we really produced something.

This was the regional office, so I worked on Guide books for four or five other states. The *Tribune* said it cost two million and wasn't worth it. No matter, they were really quite good.

The first day I went on the Project, I was frightened as much as I'd ever been in my life. My confidence had been almost destroyed in New York. I didn't know a single person here. But I found there was a great spirit of cooperation, friendliness. I discovered quickly my talents were of use.

Had been in Chicago about a month or two. I remember I wanted to buy a suit on credit. I was told nobody on the WPA could get credit in any store in Chicago. It was some years later before I could establish credit of any kind.

I bought an inexpensive radio, an Emerson. My son, David, who was four or five, dictated letters to his mother to be sent to his grandmother: "We have a radio. We bought it all ourselves. Nobody gave us it all." Apparently, he had resented that he and his mother had been living rent-free in Ohio. And she may have been getting clothes from her sister. Yeah, there was an impact even on the very young.

Do you recall the sentiments of people during the depths of the Depression?

There was a feeling that we were on the verge of a bloody revolution, up until the time of the New Deal. Many people, among them, intellectuals, without knowing what else to do, worked with the Communist Party. The Communists naturally exploited this. It began to change with the New Deal and pretty much came to an end with the Russian-German pact.

I remember a very sinking feeling during the time of the Bank Holiday. I walked down to the corner to buy a paper, giving the man a fifty-cents coin. He flipped it up in the air and said, "This is no good." And he threw it in the middle of the street. (Laughs.) Some took the Holiday as a huge joke. Others had hysteria, like this newsboy: there isn't any money, there isn't anything. Most people took it calmly. It couldn't get much worse—and something was being *done*.

Everyone was emotionally affected. We developed a fear of the future which was very difficult to overcome. Even though I eventually went into some fairly good jobs, there was still this constant dread: everything would be cut out from under you and you wouldn't know what to do. It would be even harder, because you were older. . . .

Before the Depression, one felt he could get a job even if something happened to this one. There were always jobs available. And, of course, there were always those, even during the Depression: If you wanted to work, you could really get it. Nonsense.

I suspect, even now, I'm a little bit nervous about every job I take and wonder how long it's going to last—and what I'm going to do to cause it to disappear.

I feel anything can happen. There's a little fear in me that it might happen again. It does distort your outlook and your feeling. Lost time and lost faith. . . .

VIRGINIA DURR

Wetumpka, Alabama. It is an old family house on the outskirts of Montgomery. A creek runs by. . . . She and her husband, Clifford, are of an old Alabamian lineage. During Franklin Roosevelt's Administration, he was a member of the Federal Communications Commission. She had been a pioneer in the battle to abolish the poll tax.

OH, NO, the Depression was not a romantic time. It was a time of terrible suffering. The contradictions were so obvious that it didn't take a very bright person to realize something was terribly wrong.

Have you ever seen a child with rickets? Shaking as with palsy. No proteins, no milk. And the companies pouring milk into gutters. People with nothing to wear, and they were plowing up cotton. People with nothing to eat, and they killed the pigs. If that wasn't the craziest system in the world, could you imagine anything more idiotic? This was just insane.

And people blamed themselves, not the system. They felt they had been at fault: . . . "if we hadn't bought that old radio" . . . "if we hadn't bought that old secondhand car." Among the things that horrified me were the preachers—the fundamentalists. They would tell the people they suffered because of their sins. And the people believed it. God was punishing them. Their children were starving because of their sins.

People who were independent, who thought they were masters and mistresses of their lives, were all of a sudden dependent on others. Relatives or relief. People of pride went into shock and sanitoriums. My mother was one.

Up to this time, I had been a conformist, a Southern snob. I actually thought the only people who amounted to anything were the very small group which I belonged to. The fact that my family wasn't as well off as those of the girls I went with—I was vice president of the Junior League—made me value even more the idea of being well-born. . . .

What I learned during the Depression changed all that. I saw a blinding light like Saul on the road to Damascus. (Laughs.) It was the first time I had seen the other side of the tracks. The rickets, the pellagra—it shook me up. I saw the world as it really was.

She shamed, cajoled and persuaded the dairy company into opening milk dispensaries. When they sought to back down, she convinced them that "if these people got a taste of milk, they might get in the habit of buying it—when they got jobs."

When the steel companies closed down in Birmingham, thousands were thrown out of work. She was acquainted with some of the executives; she argued with them: "You feed the mules who work in your mines. Why don't you feed the people? You're responsible."

The young today are just play-acting in courting poverty. It's all right to wear jeans and eat hamburgers. But it's entirely different from not having any hamburgers to eat and no jeans to wear. A great many of these kids—white kids—seem to have somebody in the background they can always go to. I admire their spirit, because they have a strong sense of social justice. But they themselves have not been deprived. They haven't experienced the terror. They have never seen a baby in the cradle crying of hunger. . . .

I think the reason for the gap between the black militants and the young white radicals is that the black kids are much more conscious of the thin edge of poverty. And how soon you can be reduced to living on relief. What you *know* and what you *feel* are very different. Terror is something you *feel*. When there is no paycheck coming in—the absolute, stark terror.

What frightens me is that these kids are like sheep being led to slaughter. They are romantic and they are young. I have a great deal more faith in movements that start from necessity—people trying to change things because of their own deprivation. We felt that in the labor surge of the Thirties. The people who worked hardest to organize were the ones in the shops and in the mills.

The Depression affected people in two different ways. The great majority reacted by thinking money is the most important thing in the world. Get yours. And get it for your children. Nothing else matters. Not having that stark terror come at you again. . . .

And there was a small number of people who felt the whole system was lousy. You have to change it. The kids come along and they want to change it, too. But they don't seem to know what to put in its place. I'm not so sure I know, either. I do think it has to be responsive to people's needs. And it has to be done by democratic means, if possible. Whether it's possible or not—the power of money is such today, I just don't know. Some of the kids call me a relic of the Thirties. Well, I am.